Seeing Through the Eyes of My Papa's Heart

La Marr R Wenrich

Copyright © 2013 La Marr Wenrich

All rights reserved.

ISBN: 13
978-0615783628

MY PAPA
THANK YOU FOR TEACHING ME ABOUT LOVE

LA MARR R WENRICH

I LOVE YOU.

FAITH- HOPE- LOVE

BUT THE GREATEST OF THESE IS LOVE…

SEEING THROUGH THE EYES OF MY PAPA'S HEART

ACKNOWLEDGMENTS

THERE IS NOT A GREATER GIFT IN LIFE THAN THE GIFT OF LOVE…YOU GAVE IT FREELY- UNCONDITIONALLY AND WITH ALL YOUR HEART. I LEARNED THE FIERCE LOVE OF GOD THROUGH YOUR EXAMPLE. YOUR FIGHT FOR LIFE HAS NOT GONE UNNOTICED OR BEEN IN VAIN…GIVING UP WOULD HAVE BEEN THE EASY WAY OUT BUT YOU CHOSE TO LIVE AND TO LIVE LIFE TO THE FULLEST…STANDING BY YOUR SIDE THROUGH IT ALL: MY MAMA…STRONG YET VULNERABLE, KIND BUT FIRM, BEAUTIFUL, PASSIONATE AND FULL OF LOVE. A FORCE ALL ON HER OWN--NEVER WAVERING IN HER BELIEF IN YOU. SHE SAW IN YOU WHAT YOU COULDN'T SEE IN YOURSELF. THERE ARE NO WORDS TO EXPRESS WHAT YOU TWO HAVE GIVEN ME THROUGH YOUR LOVE.

CONTENTS

1 Little Boy Lost
2 Sad Day Dawning
3 Longing for More
4 At Any Cost
5 A Brief Reprieve
6 Darkness Returns
7 Isolated
8 The Gap Widens
9 Secret Haven
10 His Moment
11 Changes
12 How Many More?
13 His Cruel Mind
14 Kindness Exists
15 Strength in Love
16 New Horizons…still the same
17 A House but not a home
18 The Madness Continues
19 A New Kind of Hurt
20 Just Another Day
21 Hope Lingers
22 Survivor
23 The Door Closes
24 At Last…

Love. Always elusive, ever changing-a mind of its' own. Love isn't tangible- though we relate it to touch, feelings, words, things. We are taught what love is by actions. It shapes us, forms us, unknowingly creating a belief in our own self worth. Love is often taken for granted until it is taken away. What if you're born into a world that is empty and without love? Even baby birds die without the touch and love of their momma. Are we able to love and give of ourselves if we are never shown love? Or is love innate, waiting inside each one of us, to be set free?

The strength of the human spirit is unexplainable. Hope--the mental willpower to keep on going....faith--believing in what you cannot see...

He slipped away...creating his own reality, a peaceful existence within a tortured mind...This lost soul without roots would spend his life seeking, craving, searching for love, acceptance and an identity...forever shaped by the cruelty of life...No one who crosses this gentle man's path would imagine that he endured such a cold, cruel and demeaning upbringing--void of love, affection or any notion of self-worth. Until the mention of his father's name...it brings him to his knees and tears flow down his cheeks unabashedly. How did he control his demons of anger, hate and vengeance that surely fumed at the surface? Was it fear that kept his emotions from spilling over, or had he always known, innately, there was more to be discovered than the cruelty he knew...a warmth and love he yearned for...

Chapter 1

Little Boy Lost

Born Arthur Felix Manuel Raymond Juan Rodriguez in a tent that was called home, a small town called Dakota, in northern California...so small and insignificant that the town no longer exists. An omen of Arthur's life to come?... Mary--a beaten down, frightened young girl became a mom to 13 children starting at the age of 12. Arthur was the fifth baby born and the only male. He would have to endure the brunt of his father's angst, abuse and torturous rage...This young boy would shoulder burdens and live through horrific situations that most people never experience or imagine in their lifetime... His odyssey began May 5th.

 Arthur is dehydrated, famished and beyond exhausted, inadequate in size and age, to haul 50 pound burlap bags of cotton through the fields. Yet his five year old body races back and forth, picking cotton, somehow placing the bag on his back, dropping it off and starting over... There are no real breaks to speak of, nor does his mind wander there. He knows he's racing time and must meet the expectations of the man that rules his world... At the end of a long day, this young boy needs to hand over a substantial amount of money to this man, his father. Arthur is paid per bag... There will be no disappointing this man. This is the norm in his life, being the only male, Arthur is expected to bring in money to feed his sisters and mom. There is no school time, friends, or playground to enjoy, not even a childhood. As far as he remembers, this is it, working in the fields and living in fear.

His father's cruelness still surprised him. Why? The innocence of a young child hanging onto hope? He wasn't sure why any of it caught him off guard, but it did. The temperatures were freezing in Santa Maria and the cold cut through to his bones. His hands were rigid and Arthur was having trouble picking the broccoli. Juan was aware of the cold coming off the coast. He brought in a big bucket of water, placed it in the middle of the fields and told the girls to dip their hands in every time they passed it, helping to ease the pain in their fingers, and take a sip of tequila to warm their bones. As Arthur approached it, Juan told him, "not you cavron(bastard), keep moving, be a man". This five year old boy bit his lip and walked on, as tears silently rolled down his red, cold cheeks. He couldn't wait until they moved on from this place.

Arthur doesn't know how long they stayed in Santa Maria, but was so grateful to hear Juan yelling at everyone to pack up. Leaving the cold, damp weather behind put a smile on his face. His spirits lifting, like only a child's could. Innocence of a child, young enough to still be naive and forgiving...shielding him from how harsh life could still be. There were many small towns they set up camps at and fields tended to, but nothing like he would have to endure later on. So much of his life is a blur. Maybe his mind protecting him from things that could only hurt. He knows they traveled from one place to another and ended up in El Paso, Texas. He has no recollection of his life before ages 4-5. He wonders though, was he ever loved and held gently like other babies he sees? Was his mom allowed to do so? Sometimes in his dreams, his momma is cradling him. He hugs her neck tightly. Than he's brought back to reality. Arthur is fairly certain she was never allowed to be affectionate and love her babies as he believes she wanted to. He feels that tug of war in her heart, he sees it when she looks longingly at him, both knowing there will never be a real mother/son relationship...

Juan Rodriguez ruled their home like a prison camp. He was a short, stocky man with dark hair, strong, thick, cruel hands and a frightening presence. He always worked for different farmers, staying busy but he drank often. Whenever he was home, the family quivered under his domination. Thoughts would race through his mind. Nothing made sense. Why? Why were they subjected to his cruelness? Was it an act of god? Could there be a god that barbaric?...One of Arthur's earlier memories was when he was about five or six. "My father was so angry because I showed emotion when he beat my momma. I don't know where he found it, but he brought in a thick leather rope. He told me not to move or cry while he beat me with it. My mom and sisters had to watch in complete silence. I was bloody all over. I resolved to never let him see any emotion from me ever again." Days later Arthur was still bruised reminding him of the consequences of crossing him.

Another incident that still haunts him to this day occurred around the age of five and lasted for about a year. Juan, always looking to make money, legally or illegally, started another business. It was a gambling/whorehouse on the border of Texas and Mexico. After working in the fields all day, Arthur was expected to work the gambling house as well. While he served sandwiches and drinks to the men and call girls, his momma also had to take care of the patrons. She collected money from the girls and made sure there was always plenty of food. At this young age, Arthur discovered how empty life can be. The atrocities he witnessed permeated his soul, tearing holes through to his core. He learned how to live in his mind and remove himself from the circumstances... "I saw anything you can imagine, from shooting up drugs to every sexual act possible. The smoke was so thick I could hardly breath. I'd shut off all people and pretend it was just a dream. I'd imagine my life was completely different. It worked while I was there, but when I got home and was finally able to go to sleep, all I could do was cry."

He couldn't quiet his mind in the silence of his home. He couldn't figure out what he had done wrong or why this man hated him so much. Arthur tried so hard to please him... Somehow he always disappointed his father. It is ugly and messy and he can't seem to get anything right. Disappointing this man was no small feat. Juan asked him to follow the work truck on one occasion and pick up the tree shavings falling out. Arthur started to do that but got distracted in his daydreams. As soon as he realized he was lost in thought, he caught his father's glare and peed his pants. Juan was livid that Arthur dare to disobey him. This five year old boy was taken home, tied up with a rope, beaten and locked in a closet. Hours later he was all but forgotten. He lost track of time. Arthur said, "I don't know what time I was put in the closet, but it was late at night when my momma was allowed to let me out. I thought they moved away and left me." Arthur was grateful to be untied. It did not matter that blood had dried on his face, arms and legs, or that he was hungry. He was relieved his family was still around.

There was never a time that this young boy didn't feel the sheer terror of being abandoned, beaten and completely left alone. It was a crippling thought, he knew he would never be enough. Arthur learned he was worthless, more of a burden, and it was crucial to prove his worth. He also knew no one gave him much thought if it wasn't work related. One time Arthur was walking home from work and saw an outhouse. Curiosity got the best of this child, lured by the luxury of a simple, crude toilet. He ran to use it and was in a hurry, always conscious of Juan thinking he was wasting time...somehow his tiny frame slipped right through the toilet. Arthur wasn't used to toilets of any kind. He always went outside and dug a hole...luckily he landed right side up. Needless to say, he was terrified! Arthur was stuck shoulder deep in poop. He screamed, yelled and cried, as spiders and a snake crawled around him. Losing his voice and hope that someone might hear him, he looked into the sky far above him, and only saw emptiness. He wondered how it could look so beautiful and lonely at the same time.

It was hours before Grandma Concha(Connie) realized he was missing and went looking for him. She could hear his screams and ran for help. Some men were able to use a rope and pull him out. Arthur says she cried and cried as she gently cleaned him. He shook for hours and couldn't shake the fear that settled in his mind. He was broken and battered. Deep down though, Arthur was stronger and tougher than he knew. Whenever a situation called for him to step up and protect his family, he was able to. Somehow, he'd muster the courage to jump in and try to stop this man from hurting his sisters. Young but protective, he would not allow fear to shut him down.

In one situation, they were all driving along the highway when Juan abruptly pulled over. He was angry with his momma Mary and pulled her out of the truck by her hair. She began screaming. The truck was alive with the shrills of the girls. Juan started beating her. Frightened for her life- Arthur jumped out of the truck bed and onto Juan's back. As he flung Arthur onto the highway, Mary, Connie and the girls screamed, fearing a car might run him over. The shrills stopped Juan in his tracks. Whenever Arthur reacted forcefully, it shocked Juan enough to mellow the situation. As quickly as Juan snapped- he would stop. He got back into the truck and drove away as if none of it happened. This responsibility would weigh heavily on Arthur. The chaos and confusion of their life really bothered him. He needed to know why Juan was so cruel. Arthur thought maybe if his momma was kind to Juan, their situation might change. He kept questioning things until he heard the rumblings of his momma's sad beginnings with this man...

Chapter 2

Sad Day Dawning

 All at once, things began to make sense. After his Grandma Connie(concha) tried explaining their situation through her tears, Arthur was sick to his stomach. He was able to answer his own angry thoughts. There was one particular question that had troubled him deeply, but never dared to ask. Arthur says he couldn't understand how his soft spoken momma would choose this man. "I'd fall asleep begging god to change this mean man, or make him disappear...and why would she let Juan be so cruel to me?" Arthur couldn't even call Juan by any term of endearment without being smacked across the face. It crushed him to discover the truth...this man was once his momma's stepfather.

Her own father disappeared in the coal mines in Oklahoma, according to Juan.

Mary's parents, Philip and Connie, lived on a big ranch with seven children, including Mary. Philip would hire ranch hands to assist him with the cattle. He had come to depend largely on Juan because he was a hard worker. When work would slow down, Philip would head out to the coal mines for extra money and take Juan with him. On this particular trip Connie became worried because Philip was gone unusually long. After many stressful days, Juan showed up alone and tells Connie that her husband is missing. She fell apart, unsure what to do with seven children and the ranch, she welcomed the help from Juan. Without spoken words or formalities, Juan stepped into Philip's shoes and took over the Feliz family. Connie would quickly discover he was nothing like her Philip. The mental, emotional and physical abuse was slow to start and by the time Connie was aware of it, she was terrified. She was still grieving for Philip and didn't know how to protect her children from this mad man she had allowed into their lives. She took the abuse in silence. All she asked was that he never harm her kids. That worked for a while.

One day Juan decided he wanted more from 9 year old Mary. His voracious appetite never satisfied. Juan always took what he wanted. Mary was one of Connie's younger children. She was shy, quiet and beautiful. Mary stuck close to her mother's side. She was helpful and always looking to please her mom. She did not like this new man in their life or the way he treated her mom. Juan told Connie to ask Mary to be kind to him and he would stop abusing her. She believed him. Juan had never been unkind to her children, only to Connie. All of this behavior was new to Connie. She had only known the gentle love of her husband Philip. Unaware of his real intentions and desperate to end the beatings- she asked her daughter to stop ignoring Juan and treat him kindly. Mary agreed and befriended this man. Juan went out of his way to gain her trust. Life became peaceful for a moment, even the beatings stopped. Mother and daughter were both pleased. After a few months, Connie nor Mary would ever recognize their lives again.

He took Mary, along with her mom Connie and disappeared from the life he had created with them in Oklahoma. They were dragged into his madness. As they were driving away, Mary looked out the back window waving bye with a sinking feeling in her gut. Mary nor Connie ever saw their family again. Mary left behind six siblings. Shortly after moving far away from the life she knew, Mary was forced to become Juan's lover at around age 10 while her mom was his wife. The battle she put up was fierce in the beginning. Her mom Connie also tried to stop him. After Mary watched Juan almost kick her mom to death, she stopped fighting him. She allowed Juan to have his way with her anytime he pleased without a fight. It suffocated the life out of her.

Together, Mary and Connie would both bear his children for several years. Until Juan decided he was done with Connie, but never allowed her to leave. Connie gave birth to two children from Juan, than became the housekeeper and cook. She had to endure not only being abused and beaten, but watch and hear him rape & beat her young, beautiful Mary. Connie became the nursemaid to Mary's 13 children, as well as the two she had with Juan, while Mary was forced to work in the fields. This horrible cycle continued for the rest of Juan's life. As Arthur grew and understood the dynamics between his grandma, momma and Juan, he became enraged. He had to find ways to channel his anger into something better than vengeance... "I became more determined than ever to work harder and protect momma and Grandma Concha(connie) from this man. I would somehow stop this man from harming us." He was terrified of his father, and didn't know how he'd accomplish his new goal.

The one thing he knew with certainty was that this man was much more capable than just hate. One night while serving patrons at the gambling house Arthur overheard men arguing. He stood on his tippy toes trying to see who it was. Everyone towered over this little five year old boy. He crawled between the customers until he reached the voices across the room. Arthur saw a man yelling, inches from Juan's face. Horrified, he watched his father take a gun out of his pant pocket and hold it to this strangers body. Arthur screamed "no" and went running toward the men. The sound of the gun going off stopped him cold. Everyone scattered, leaving quickly. The man fell face first landing next to Arthur. He couldn't stop his body from shaking. His father had shot and killed a man in the gambling house in a dispute over money. His one true love-- money. The root of all evil. Arthur charged at Juan crying and yelling "why?"... Juan dragged him out the back door and gave him a beating. He than told him to stop crying and help him close up. This murder ended life as Arthur knew it...not imagining it could be worse.

They would have to survive while hiding from the law. As his family was packing up and sneaking off in the dark, Arthur wondered what would become of that man bleeding on the floor in the gambling house. He did his best to erase that image from his mind. His life on the run began. Juan decided they'd go to Juarez, Mexico. He'd be safe from the law and could start searching for his mother. He had not seen her since age 12 and heard she may be in Juarez. No one knew anything about Juan's family or his background, only that he was found wandering alone and homeless around the age11 or 12. What happened to him? Arthur asked his grandma many times why he was abandoned. Had Juan lost his soul at this age? Was it only fair to destroy Mary at the same age? It's believed that his family all died during the influenza epidemic. Now Juan would force his family to wander place to place, always seeking refuge for rest and safety. Arthur would soon realize that life could always be worse...he would learn quickly how to be a survivor in all situations.

The change in Arthur's young life was swift and unexpected. He was well aware that his father was running for his life. They were all being dragged along not because he wanted or loved them, but rather he needed them. A means to an end. Arthur, than around six, recalls feeling conflicted about whether he hoped Juan was caught or not. He dared to dream that his father might have a change of heart and love them in this new life that was unfolding. The gift of hope. The innocence of a child- so quick to forget and forgive... As life went on, Arthur concluded that he would have been better off if Juan had been captured.

While Juan's uncontrollable anger had tormented the family for years, this man on the run was even more obsessively controlling than before. He was cruel and angry. Arthur would listen to Mary feebly ask Juan to stop so she could find food and feed the starving kids. He never gave them a thought, driving for hours at a time with no bathroom breaks, food or water. He'd respond to her with a swift slap to her cheek. Juan had them traveling in the back of workers trucks, hitching rides to the next farm. They would settle there, usually in the open fields, for as long as there was work. Juan would make sure everyone knew that Mary and the girls were untouchable. He had a reputation for being mean, crazy and fearless. His own childhood sufferings clearly irreparable. It had infected his whole life. No one crossed his path. There was such a dichotomy with this man.

Juan was able to get work anywhere he went. The farmers treated him with respect and fear. Arthur found it confusing. So many unanswered questions...he wondered why no one stopped Juan from hurting them. It wasn't a secret. How could it be? Arthur knew the whole town must hear Juan beating him. Yet, this man did keep their private lives very private. They were instructed to never speak of the going ons at home. Juan left no doubt of the price they would pay for opening their mouths. He never let anyone know what really went on behind closed doors. Juan was manipulative and got whatever he wanted. Arthur found it odd that Juan wanted them protected from the field workers but abused them himself...

Though he accepted there were things he simply wouldn't understand, it grieved him. Arthur watched Juan's evil ways and hated this man. He wished Juan would get sick and die like his family had. Than changing his mind as he often would, Arthur would panic at the thought of Juan leaving them. He wondered who would take care of them? Arthur knew he didn't like his father but believed he needed him. He was curious why he didn't feel guilty for disliking him. But he understood that this man was not good to him. After long days of work, more often than not, there was no food or place to sleep. Juan would show up drunk and slap Arthur around, angry that his son didn't have food for the family. He'd scream, "you better keep everyone safe, feed them and be ready for work in the morning", as he walked out the door. Juan would take the hard earned money to go gamble and drink. Though hungry and tired, Arthur and his family breathed a sigh of relief every time he left. But they had better have a camp site set up for his return.

Arthur was definitely optimistic. He never wanted his grandma or momma to worry, assuring them he would find a camp. Off he'd go looking for places to settle for the night. Eager to please them, Arthur would find trees and hang sheets from them. Than this dirt-stained, skinny, determined little boy would race back to his family to show them their new home. Connie(grandma concha) would sweep the dirt, evening out the ground. This would become their makeshift home. While Arthur and Connie were busy putting the home together, Mary(momma) was looking for food. She would show up with oranges and create anything she could think of. Arthur was very resourceful. He'd follow the running water looking for anything edible, and race back to the camp to share the guppies he'd caught. This family was so hungry they were never picky. Mary would also cook up tumbleweeds. She would find safe spots for the kids to go to the restroom during the night. There would be no showers or running water to speak of for days, sometimes weeks. It was times like this that they'd all find reasons to laugh. Mary and Connie were also creative. Connie would decorate tumbleweeds as Christmas trees to put a smile on the children's faces, while Mary would tell wild ghost stories to occupy their minds. It was a much needed distraction from the daily fear and hunger they always felt. Laughter wasn't allowed when Juan was around. His pride wouldn't allow it. He assumed they were laughing at him. There was a sense of normalcy with him gone, even in the midst of such hard times. Mary would tell Arthur and the girls to imagine they were eating stew, soup and meat. He would do just that. Arthur said, "I'd take my food, walk out into the fields, lay down and count the stars. I'd feel peaceful. I wondered if there was really a god up there that loved me. I kept hearing that from my mom. But I wasn't sure if she was just trying to comfort us, or if she actually believed it... I've spent a lifetime alone, or so it seems to me. I was looking for something to believe in."

Chapter 3

Longing for More

 As they worked and traveled like vagabonds from field to field, Mary looked out for her children best she could. There was not a regular routine or schedule for this family other than work. As a result, Mary and Connie struggled to find a balance of any kind for their brood. Life was so uncertain in Juarez, Mexico. Arthur disliked everything about it. One of the things that terrified him was the rain. Their camp was next to a river called Rio de Rojo. Anytime it rained, the river became a raging mass of water. It flooded everywhere and washed away anything in its path--cattle, cars, shacks, even people. It didn't discriminate. Arthur would go to his grandma for comfort. He was starting to notice his momma was becoming increasingly uncomfortable with his presence. She'd make him kneel down with her as she prayed and cried. She was also terrified that the waters would take them as it rose and surrounded their camp. They were alone. Juan never seemed to be around when there was danger. To comfort them, Mary would speak of this god that was watching and protecting them. Anytime the opportunity arose, Mary would find a church and sneak to it with the kids. Arthur never questioned the teachings, or why they would sneak off to these different churches. He didn't even ask why they weren't really being protected. When he'd find himself groping along, desperately hanging on, he would choose to believe. Arthur fiercely needed to hope there was someone capable of saving them. He was also realizing that his mom was as frightened of their life as he was.

Once the family was done working and settling in for the night, Arthur and Mary's second job began. There was not much rest mentally or physically for these two weary souls. They took turns keeping watch over the girls and Grandma Connie. Mary kept a big knife under her pillow. Arthur always wondered where she got that knife... Their makeshift homes were always surrounded by drunk field workers. Arthur lived in fear of these men when darkness came upon them. He was well aware of how violent a drunk man could become. This young boy was starting to see his father in most men. He learned to exist on two to three hours of sleep.

Arthur said it would seem impossible to ever escape this man. "To this day I catch myself becoming that lost little boy. It gives me that horrible feeling in the pit of my stomach. I struggle with loneliness even while surrounded by love. I know the feeling of loneliness is just in my head, but at times it seems impossible to shake. I'm back in those fields--alone, frightened and fighting for my life." Arthur has to work to keep his past buried and his mind clear. But those thoughts are always looming at the surface.

Everyday was more or less the same. Once he was in the fields working, he felt somewhat safe. Arthur was picked on at the camps they lived at for not speaking Spanish, but at work he was an equal and treated the same. This child somehow found the positive in his circumstances. As hard as this work was, he preferred it to sitting still. He felt in control of his young life while picking cotton. Juan was also not around...He'd like to dream that he would own fields like these one day and take care of his momma, grandma & sisters. Arthur's greatest desire was to have his very own family. His very own anything... He couldn't quite imagine that, but it was all he thought of. To this day when he talks about it, tears still roll softly down his face without him being aware of it..."I just knew I had to believe having something of my own--an animal, a wife, children--

they would take away the empty feeling I always had. I'd belong to someone and they'd want me."

The concept of being wanted was foreign to Arthur. "Growing up, I was unwanted by my father and tolerated by my momma. I never carried on a meaningful conversation with Juan. Nor did he ever show any affection toward me. The only physical contact he ever displayed were the beatings he'd give me. Though I was grateful for every moment he wasn't hurting me, I didn't want to be hated anymore." As it became painfully clear that this was going to be his life, the more Arthur craved love and acceptance. The mystery of it all. This fueled his dreams of having something more.

Perhaps it was the very dream of having more and protecting his family that somehow kept Arthur focused. Hours turned into days, weeks and months. He was still moving place to place following the work. His sisters were getting older, becoming young women. It was becoming more and more difficult to protect them from the restless field workers. Arthur kept his ears and eyes open, always paying attention. There were times that he'd have to step in and tell the men to leave his sisters alone. Though Arthur was undernourished and diminutive, small and thin for his age, he'd take on anyone who wouldn't listen. Many times he'd take a beating, but Arthur felt good accomplishing his goal. When it was all said and done, Arthur would question himself on why he felt so good about this. Did it fill his emptiness? He never could figure out if he did it for his sisters' safety or his own...the consequences he would have to endure if harm came to the girls under his watch scared him to death.

It wasn't just the physical protection of the girls that kept Arthur on his feet, it was also feeding them that he struggled with...work was scarce and they didn't stay put long enough for any rancher to see their value. So Arthur was always looking for ways to make extra money or steal food. Luck was on his side, wild asparagus grew all around, which became their staple. He'd leave their camp all alone and walk around looking for anything he could do for food. Most nights, Arthur would sneak into the small stores around the different camps and grab anything his little hands could hold. One afternoon as he was attempting to steal from a food cart, an older gentleman caught his eye. This man was looking at him much the way he'd look at his momma, sorrow and sadness interwoven...he waved Arthur over and asked him if he'd like to earn some money and food. He let Arthur unload the back of his truck. It was filled with coal. Several men were also helping out. This kind man gave Arthur a bagful of food, as well as money. He ran all the way back to camp, black with soot from head to toe. Arthur says, "I can't even explain the sheer joy and happiness I felt running home, knowing I could take care of my family." He said when Grandma Connie saw him, she hugged him and gently wiped away his tears. His resentment dissipated, giving way to gratitude. Arthur wished finding work and food was always this easy.

Chapter 4

At Any Cost

As they traveled and followed work deeper into Mexico, it was apparent that it was very dangerous for the girls. Prostitution was rampant. While Arthur and Mary were diligent and successful in protecting the girls from the pimps, Juan was a different story. He had other ideas. Their father was aware the girls had been approached about selling their bodies for sex. Juan decided it would be another way to make money. Arthur said Mary and Connie started putting a plan together immediately to get them out of there. Mary Feliz, a beautiful young woman with long, red hair was starting to show the pain of the life she lived on her face. Dark circles under her bright blue eyes, hung heavy and thick, understanding all to well the suffering her children were forced to endure.

In order to travel place to place through Mexico, they needed their papers/birth certificates. Connie was in charge of these very important documents. Somehow the papers were misplaced. During a heated argument between Mary and Juan, she announced that the papers were missing. Mary let him know she was taking the kids and leaving because they weren't safe without them. Though Juan started acting crazy and threatening her, she did not back down. Mary screamed, "you can beat me up, but unless you kill me, you won't stop me from leaving." All at once it was silent. Arthur says something clicked in Juan's mind. He stared at Mary and Connie standing arm in arm, which was unusual, looked at all the kids and shrugged his shoulders. He looked unsure of himself for the first time that Arthur could remember. It was as if he knew this was a fight he couldn't win.

Arthur was full of emotions he wasn't used to. His heart beating wildly. He not only felt a sense of pride for his mom, but he felt protected. It didn't escape him that this fight was about the girls, but nonetheless he allowed himself to be a part of it all. He was excited, hopeful and ready for a new start. Within a matter of days, Connie and Arthur had packed up their humble belongings. Things were set and ready when Juan walked in and said, "Mary you can take the older girls, but Connie, Arthur, Vivian, Joey and the babies stay with me. I need them for work. We will meet you where ever you end up at." Arthur was crushed. His momma once again let her voice be heard. Mary said that was fine, except she was taking her son. She used the excuse of needing him for safety. So it was settled. Arthur always wondered if she really needed him, or just wanted him... after all, she left behind three toddlers and her infant Rosa. Once he knew they were really leaving Juan behind, Arthur exhaled. He was tired. Weary. Anxious. Afraid. He quietly hoped Juan would never meet them anywhere. The long trek home began. Where would that be exactly was the question in Arthur's mind...

The long journey home was not an easy one. Arthur says they were mostly hungry and very tired. Yet the mood was lighthearted. "It was the first time I can remember that we laughed out loud," Arthur said. "We didn't look around to make sure Juan couldn't hear us, we talked freely. That may sound trivial, but the feeling is hard to explain. Talking was a privilege for us and we were treasuring every moment of it." Laughing was a much needed distraction on this trip. When there was no transportation available, this family of a young mom, six girls and seven year old Arthur would walk for hours without a break. Hunger, weather or exhaustion were not given much thought. They were racing time. Arthur had to take care of all these girls and he carried the burden mentally, emotionally and physically.

The food supply was running low. Mary and Arthur had packed up as much food as they could carry, but it wasn't much. Arthur knew that food was necessary, in order for the girls to keep walking. They had gone hungry many nights before, but were at least sleeping in their tent homes. Only Arthur was used to going a day or two with no real food and working hard. This was different altogether. No food, no work and no place to sleep. The sleeping conditions were not a problem. The kids were used to sleeping anywhere their whole lives. The whole gang would gather closely together on the floor/ground for warmth and fall asleep. Arthur did what he must for food. When nighttime came, he'd sneak off and steal food. He would grab whatever he could, as fast as he could and sprint back to the family. His was heart racing, terrified of being caught and abandoning the girls. The unspoken responsibility was his alone. Mary found every cotton farm she could, and though they worked as much as possible, Arthur shouldered the brunt of it all.

Sometimes the pressure was more than he could bear. He'd lay his head where ever he could to rest and cry. He really missed his Grandma Concha--his nickname for her. She was the only one to show Arthur any affection. It didn't matter that it wasn't that often, Arthur knew she cared. He'd study her and wondered often, how sad she must be that she married Juan. She was kind, gentle and didn't deserve him. Connie fought to protect Arthur. After all, he was still a young boy. Connie would be the only person in his young life to show Arthur that he mattered. She'd do that by hugging him when she could, sneaking a piece of bread to him or just a sweet smile... His momma, on the other hand, remained closed off emotionally and rather cold to him. There was a problem between Mary and Connie too. His momma was mean to his grandma. Arthur was angry at his mom, but could always sense her sadness. He was wise beyond his years. Intuitively, he knew she must have a special love for him. Arthur believed if she allowed her emotions to surface, she wouldn't know how to stop the tears...so he too would turn off his emotions. This would become a part of his inner being for the rest of his days. Angry or not, he never wanted his momma to hurt because of him. He was more determined than ever to get them safely to their new destination....where ever that was to be.

Every step, every mile, every new town put more distance between them and Juan. They traveled through Brollo, Indio and any farming community they could find. This family was a sight to see. A beautiful young woman with a handful of young, dirty children. It was rare to see this, especially without a male to protect them. They moved around like gypsies. It was tedious, hard field work. The weather was unrelenting, be it cold or hot. Mary had become anxious, exhausted and mean. Her frustrations were aimed at Arthur. She worried about the children she left behind, as well as the brood with her. Mary was scared and very uncertain about her future. The children could sense her angst, and the kids became very close during this time. Arthur said they realized they had no one except one another. A very tight bond was formed between these siblings. He said, "it was us against the world." Arthur had no idea this bond that saved him would cause such pain throughout his life. For now, all he understood was they needed each other and he needed to work harder to protect them.

This little spitfire was a sight to behold. He moved twice the speed of men much older than him while picking cotton. There was talk of this homeless family, and the little boy who never seemed to rest. It was how Arthur functioned best. His nervous energy didn't allow him to sit still anymore. He had to come realize his only value was in his work. Mary was pleased with his work ethic. They were able to keep moving northbound, slowly but surely, following the seasons through the farmlands. Arthur had become adept at any form of fieldwork. He not only worked at picking cotton, he also worked the onion, corn and tomato fields. Mary had made it known that the better workers they were, the quicker she could send for the other kids. Arthur wondered if Juan would come with them...

Chapter 5

A Brief Reprieve

Somehow Juan was able to keep track of them. Mary knew it was very important for Juan to hear how hard they were working. His presence was everywhere. Arthur never questioned anything anymore. He did agonize over why they couldn't just disappear and never see Juan again. It was disappointing to hear that he knew their whereabouts. Yet, Arthur was definitely anxious to see Grandma Connie....he didn't know what the future had in store for him, but he rarely thought about the next day. He only knew he wanted to live, not like his father walking lifelessly, but fully live. After many months of traveling, Mary came upon a gold mine, Edison Highway, as far as field work is concerned. They had ended up on the outskirts of the infamous grapevine. Who would've known this unlikely place would be the vicinity of where this Rodriguez Family would finally set down roots.

Arthur thought it all looked the same. They were surrounded by farmlands. He couldn't understand why his momma was so excited. Mary rarely showed any emotion at all, so he knew it must be important. After she was done talking to this man, Gabby, she let the family know that they would be able to stay here indefinitely. He owned the land as far as the eye could see. There would be work all year around--potatoes, onions, tomatoes, corn, grapevines, oranges and almond trees--all to be picked. Arthur stared at his momma. She looked tired, sad and relieved. He would've given anything to know what she really thought and how she really felt. There were tears running down her face and he wanted to hug her, but he didn't know how. As always, she looked at him as if she knew just what he was thinking. Mary attempted a smile with her lifeless eyes before she walked away. Arthur never felt more alone. Luckily, or not, he naturally buried his feelings. Arthur's thoughts were already focused on this man they'd be working for. He trusted no one, especially men. However, Gabby would prove to be a different kind of man, allowing Arthur to let his guard down a little.

Within a matter of days, this destitute family was setting up house. In the middle of this beautiful orchard-sat a rather large one room adobe. It was about as perfect as anything Arthur could imagine.

He couldn't believe their luck. They would have a real roof, doors and a floor...Gabby helped Arthur replace broken windows, doors and put up shelves. He also felt bad that it wasn't bigger or filled with furniture. This house didn't have the usual amenities a home has. There were no bedrooms, beds or sofas, but no one was complaining. Arthur and his family slept on the floor, as usual, except the dirt was missing. He watched his momma still put the knife next to her, but she relaxed. He tried to still his thoughts and do the same. They actually both slept through the night. Upon awakening, Arthur says he smiled. The nightmare of his life had taken a turn. It was sinking in that this man might not hurt them. This seven year old boy was worry-free for the first time in his life.

The family adjusted easily and settled in. There was much work to be done. Arthur had taken over these fields, putting his heart, mind and soul into his work. He proved himself to be invaluable. After watching this family work for months in his orchards and fields, Gabby really appreciated them. One day he noticed Arthur scratching incessantly. He told Arthur that he had chicken pox. He explained that he was going to tie his hands and have him rest. Arthur was so disappointed for believing in Gabby, assuming this was some form of punishment. Instead, Gabby gently cleansed the pox that had become sores and put a cream over them. Arthur understood than, that this was a labor of love. He happily allowed his hands to be tied to prevent anymore scratching, and couldn't think of a time he felt more cared for than that moment. Though Gabby was a busy rancher, he always took the time to check in on them. Gabby made sure there was food to eat and that they were warm at night. He tried to engage Arthur in conversation and get to know them. Arthur says he worried about his family. "He'd never ask directly how or why we ended up on Edison Highway, but I knew he wanted to know. He really wanted to help us. I told him I couldn't say a thing or I'd get beat by Juan. Gabby didn't push the issue anymore, but he had that same sad look in his eyes that momma always had." Arthur says it was at times like this that he knew they'd never be free from Juan. The man was nowhere to be seen, yet his presence was suffocating. Arthur felt shaken, undone, hopeless. He took a deep breath, his lungs filling up and deflating slowly...ridding the poison from his soul, emotions under control now...

Life was going smoothly for this dysfunctional family. In any other, ordinary simple life of most people, they would be appalled at the existence of this Rodriguez family... The dysfunction was deeply rooted. It was as normal as breathing. The fact that this family could run, hide or ask Gabby for help but wouldn't, leaves no doubt how normal the craziness was. Mary nor the older girls tried to change or resist their way of life. Terror and fear pulsed through their veins as freely as blood does. It was a way of life. They wouldn't dare challenge any of Juan's rules, though he was hundreds of miles away. Arthur knew that some of them must have endured horrible moments with the man. Juan would take one sister or another at different times into a room. The silence angered Arthur. Was the door locked? It didn't matter, he was to afraid to go and check. Arthur desperately wanted to save his sisters from the wrath of Juan. He knew the girls wanted him to do something by the silent looks they gave him. They understood though, no one opened a door that Juan closed, nor was there ever a discussion about what went on in that room. Arthur knew secrets were meant to be buried and forgotten. He obeyed. In spite of all this, without the stress, pressure and fear of Juan around life seemed perfect. This young boy had no complaints. He would tell you that he was even grateful, hopeful and praying for his new life to never change.

The only thing missing was Grandma Concha(Connie). Arthur really wanted to see her and feel the warmth of another human being. But the thought of more mouths to feed and less room in the adobe-would he be kicked to the outside to sleep? It also frightened him to imagine facing Juan again everyday. It was more than he could bear. Yes, he secretly hoped that things would remain the same for a long time to come. For a short while, his wish was granted.

Time stands still for no one. As he was walking to the adobe from the orchards, his older sister ran to him. She was out of breath, as she excitedly yelled out, "The family is back! Momma is going to pick them up!" Her expression couldn't hide the horror of what those words meant to all of them. Arthur's heart skipped a beat and he could feel his world slipping away once again. He continued walking toward the spot his family had all gathered at. Mary was standing there with her hands on her hips, trying to look calm. She was sadness wearing a smile. Arthur knew her to well and the tension in her face couldn't be quieted... He was immediately hurting for her beautiful, sad, blue eyes. Though she had to be cold to them in order to survive, particularly to Arthur, he could always feel her thoughts. It was crushing to this young child. Mary quietly announced, "I'm going to meet the family and bring them back here. Mijo you're in charge of everyone while I'm gone." Anytime Mary called Arthur 'mijo', he hurt all the more for everything they weren't.

Arthur was surprised his momma wasn't excited to pick up the children, especially her infant Rita. She had been so anxious about them early on. He knew she must feel like he did. Juan came along with the package. There was already a thick layer of tension looming over them. As Mary turned around to leave, Arthur walked toward her wanting to give her a hug. Instead, his momma gave him that empty smile and got into some man's truck and left. He felt utterly alone.

Arthur took off running to the orchards. He was so angry and confused about everything. He found solace in these quiet, beautiful fields. This lost little boy was mad at his momma. His thoughts overwhelming him...Why couldn't she stop this?

Why couldn't she protect him? Didn't she know how scared he was again? His life was a twisted nightmare. He hoped none of them came back... Guilt enveloped him. Arthur hated being angry, especially at his momma. He tried so hard to have no emotions for her at all, and almost always succeeded at this. The rare times his love for his momma surfaced, it took his breath away. Mary never responded to him and it terrified him. Questions loomed in his mind and he couldn't shut them out. Did she love him at all? The loneliness was daunting. Arthur says, "I fell to my knees and asked that god to help me. But I was sure he couldn't hear me either." Nevertheless, he cried to the skies.

He started to relax a little and lied down in the fields. With his eyes closed, Arthur started daydreaming. This was his escape and he relished the moments. He was awake in this dream and not wanting to die. Carefree and child-like, playing with friends. There was no Juan and he was fearless. Arthur imagined his momma loved him, hugging him as he got ready for school. Oh how he wished he could really go to school... His tears startled him back to reality. How long had he been there? He ran furiously back to the house, terrified of what awaited him...

As he came around the corner, nearing the adobe, his little sisters saw him. They squealed with delight and ran up to him, hugging him. It surprised him and he hugged them tightly. Most surprising to him was how he felt. Arthur rarely felt any emotion toward another human being. He gave in to it for a moment. But only for a moment, his thoughts consumed by the presence of Juan. He wondered where he was as he walked around the house. Arthur followed his momma's voice and started running toward it when he realized it was Grandma Connie he was hearing...

Once again, his emotions caught him off guard. Arthur was shocked as he threw himself into Connie's arms and cried. He couldn't control himself. It was as if his body had a mind of its' own... As she was consoling him, he quickly remembered why she was there. Juan had brought her back, but not for him. Arthur cautiously straightened up and pushed away from his grandma and looked for Juan. He was shocked to see Vivian and Joey standing there. He turned toward Mary and asked, "where is he?" A wave of relief flooded over him as she shook her head no. Not quite sure what that meant except that Juan was no where in sight, Arthur understood that to be good news. Or was it? As panic set in, he asked timidly, "are you sending me to him?" Connie and Mary both told him no. Connie went on to explain that Juan had lost his traveling papers and couldn't leave Mexico. She also said it would take time for him to attain the papers, but he would be joining them soon. Arthur was no longer listening, but excitedly dragging his grandma to the adobe to show her their new home.

This family was once again settling back into life, with a much fuller household. Connie had not only brought back the four toddlers, but also her two children with Juan, Vivian and Joey. Though these two children existed, they were hardly seen and certainly not heard. Arthur often wondered where his cousins-as he referred to them as-had been...Who took care of them? Why weren't they allowed to live with them? He did ask his sisters off and on about them. The only thing Arthur was told was that there had been a big fight about Connie's children and than they were gone. All of it broke Arthur's heart for his Grandma Connie, Mary and his half siblings. He refused to let his mind dwell on that, but he was determined to find out why they were here now.

As usual, no one was talking. His momma and grandma were silent on the subject. Arthur couldn't find out why these two showed up with Connie. He decided he'd ask Joey and Vivian himself. Joey told him that Connie brought them back because Juan almost killed him. Arthur wasn't shocked but he was. Joey was told to protect Vivian while Juan was gone. She ended up cutting herself and there was blood everywhere. When Juan came back and saw it, he went crazy. Juan might have beat Joey to death, if not for Vivian begging and screaming for him to stop. It was decided than that they'd travel back with Connie, their mom. Arthur could not understand why this man hated them so much. He hoped this man never came back. Arthur showed Joey and Vivian around the orchard and introduced them to Gabby. Though he was happy to have them back, they were not very happy to be there. Arthur wasn't sure why there was so much tension between them and his older sisters. But life went on and they all managed to work and live together. He was just thrilled that they all squeezed into this adobe, all 15 of them, and no one had to sleep outside.

Several months went by before anyone mentioned Juan. Arthur cherished every moment of it. When he wasn't working, he was enjoying hanging out with Joey. He started asking his grandma about going to school, asking turned into begging. Connie had a soft spot for her mijo, and she broached the subject with Mary. At first she said no. Than Arthur asked her, "if I keep working after school, can I please try it out?" He was relentless, never taking no for an answer. A trait that has worked well for Arthur throughout his life. He said she softened to the idea and allowed him to give it a try. Mary was adamant though, that he would work as diligent and hard as he always had. So began a new phase in Arthur's life.

He was so excited. Arthur wasn't sure what to expect. The fact that he had to go work the fields at 5 a.m. did not dampen his enthusiasm. He had never been to school and couldn't wait to leave. As soon as he completed what his momma expected, he put on the nicest clothes he owned, grabbed the lunch made and packed by Connie and was off. There was no big fanfare, or excited hugs and well wishes for his first day of school, just grandma waving bye. Gabby had lent Arthur a bicycle to get himself to school. He also let the school know to expect this young boy. Arthur says it was a great experience. He was anxious to please and work hard. His teacher was patient and tried to teach him letters and numbers. Ms. Miller was surprised when she realized he had never been taught anything at age eight.

Arthur knew his teacher was kind. He'd watch her interact with all the children, wondering how she knew how to love them all. She tried reaching out to Arthur often, and he warmed up to her, but refused to tell her about his family. He did promise to learn all the things he didn't know. Ms. Miller kept her eyes on him, aware that things were certainly not okay. A bond grew between these two and Arthur wanted to make her proud of him. He was enjoying school and all it offered. He loved being around kids his age. Most of the students were nice to him, though it was obvious he was a couple of years older. As hard as Arthur worked at school, he had to work harder in the fields before and after school. It was taking a toll on this young boy and he'd fall asleep in class. Ms. Miller just kept on trying to teach him how to read and write. The discipline he needed in order to learn this, was not supported at home. There were to many mouths to feed and much work to be done. Nevertheless, Arthur rose at 3:30 a.m., worked the fields and jumped on that bike every morning, excited to go to school. His teacher continued to praise Arthur, though he wasn't able to retain the things she was teaching him.

Chapter 6

Darkness Returns

After a few months of attending school, Arthur told his Grandma Connie that he wasn't sure what he was learning, but he liked it all. She was proud of how hard her grandson was working. She tried to make sure he always knew that. She made a point of being outside any chance she could for his arrival. As he rode up on his bike on this particular day, he was smiling and waving. It grieved her to have to let him know that Juan had sent word. He couldn't get his papers in order, so he would be traveling with a group of people on foot and boat to reach them. Arthur's expression said all he didn't dare express. He would turn pale white all around his mouth whenever he was nervous. There would be no chatter about school on this day. Instead, Arthur went straight to the orchards and started working. His Grandma Concha's sad face didn't escape him. He said, "I felt bad taking it out on her, like it was her fault. But I couldn't help it. I needed to run and escape to the fields, or I felt like I'd go crazy. I was angry because even she couldn't protect me. I wondered if any of the kids I met at school had father's like mine..." Perhaps Arthur kept fleeing, trying to outrun the pain that was pursuing him.

As usual, one day slipped into the next. Everything was always the same--work, school and more work.

Arthur couldn't help but notice one thing that was changing. His two oldest sisters were maturing and their looks were changing. He thought this might infuriate Juan. They looked as old as their momma Mary. Of course, he was to young to put it all together. The age difference was minuscule between Mary and her oldest daughter, barely 11 & 1/2 years. Arthur said he was older when he realized that his momma was a very young girl having kids...it made him sick to his stomach. He felt an icy-cold rage pulsate through his body every time he thought about it. He taught himself to breathe and just kept moving, in order to keep his soul from atrophying...Life went on.

There was quite a commotion going on outside the adobe as Arthur approached it. He knew what it meant and walked as slow as possible. Gabby joined him, trying to engage Arthur in conversation. He asked him, "are you ready to see Juan? I met him and he thanked me for employing his family." Arthur didn't respond and tried wiping away the tears that kept rolling down his cheeks...it was as if they had a mind of their own. He hated how his body betrayed him. Gabby told Arthur he could help him, but Arthur only shook his head no. They walked on in silence. Arthur's heart beat wildly.

Juan was checking out everyone. All the were girls lined up alongside Connie and Mary, including Vivian and Joey. Arthur could hear his remarks, half English, half Spanish...commenting on how grown up they looked. This was not a happy reunion. It was a master overlooking his slaves or property. A couple of the younger girls looked excited, or was it fear? His oldest sister, Donna, was definitely angry. She had become quite vocal with his absence. Donna let it be known that she would not allow him to hurt her again. He wasn't sure she'd be that brave now that Juan was here...it didn't really matter. Arthur is immobilized by the horrible thoughts flooding his mind. Had his mind failed him? Letting him down-as everyone else had? The details of the madness of life with this man eluded him once again-until now... They say memory is shocked back to life with trauma's electricity. He knew there was nothing to be done. They'd be devoured once again by Juan.

This man loomed larger than life. Arthur caught himself gasping for breath. Why? He told himself to keep working hard and please his father. All he really wanted to do was curl up in a ball and hug his legs, warding off the evil that he felt strangling him. No matter that the noose was being tightened on his life. Arthur reminded himself that he was a fighter, a survivor and would not give up. He couldn't. Juan stood over him, always angry to see him. Arthur quivered in his skin--the faceless, voiceless boy. "Tell me why you're going to school?!" his voice boomed. It reverberated in Arthur's head. "I knew I needed to speak. My silence would be my own undoing...my tongue couldn't move. My mouth felt full of cotton and I was parched." Juan lunged at him, and Arthur didn't move. He barely even flinched. It was as if Arthur accepted free falling back into Juan's madness. Connie physically stopped him. Unconcerned for herself, she became his guardian angel. She stepped in between them and took the blows meant for Arthur. The whole family is up with the chaos. Terror filled eyes, grief stricken souls, yet silent. Mary spoke. Arthur says she was barely audible as she said, "I gave him permission and he will finish up this year. He is still working." There was something about Mary that could silence Juan, once in a while. Though his voice was quieted, he couldn't resist pummeling Arthur as he walked out. Is that what Juan needed to feel good about himself? Was he crazy? Or was he to, in need of something to believe in, besides himself?

As the sun was rising to say good morning, so to were Arthur and Juan. The frightened boy was back-overtaking Arthur's mind. He was moving as quickly and quietly as his heavy-laden feet would move. Everything was different now. The adobe was no longer a home. Where would his refuge be? Time was once again his enemy. If he moved to slow, he was lazy...to fast, he was doing an incomplete job. Arthur was out the door and running to the orchards before Juan could utter a word to him. He ran wildly. Tears everywhere, much like his thoughts. The sun, the smells and feel of the crops were soothing to his heart, mind and soul. Arthur gave in to it. It nourished him. Soon he was finishing up and on his way to school. He never looked back, pedals flying as he raced to school. Grateful for the reprieve.

Juan made his presence known. He was the force in charge. It was only a matter of days before his methods permeated their home, the orchards, their lives...the simple life they had managed to create was withering away, like a plant slowly drowning...Mary was under his control again. Again? Had she ever been free? Not that he could remember...A stench of death hung over them. Juan liked the work the orchards offered, it kept his family busy and bringing in the money. He did not like sharing power with another man-not even when he was good to them. This thought gnawed at him like an open wound festering. It kept Juan busy. He was searching for a new place to live and work. Arthur was thankful for that. It no longer mattered to him where they lived, chaos was back and terror reared it's ugly head. Spring was in the air, school was coming to a close and changes were upon them.

The ability to accept changes, good or bad, is not an easy task for most people. Arthur would falter, but only for a moment. He made the most of each moment, acutely aware that life was unpredictable. Juan kept his eyes on everything, sucking the life out of each thing he touched...He kept his distance from Gabby as he'd stroll the orchards checking on the girls and Arthur working. He did let Gabby know that they'd be moving on soon. One afternoon Gabby caught up with Arthur, as he was dropping his bike on the dirt road, scurrying to work. Arthur liked his company and missed seeing him lately. He noticed Gabby stayed away since Juan's arrival.

Who wouldn't? Arthur said it was like living on a deserted island since Juan returned. Silence was everywhere. No more laughter. No hugs or smiles from Grandma Connie. Even school lost its' luster. Just silence. Gabby's 'hello' was a welcomed sound to a starving soul.

Gabby wanted to let Arthur know that he was proud of how hard he worked in school and the orchards. He also told him that he'd miss him around. Arthur liked hearing those words, but he felt nothing. Would he miss Gabby? Was he proud of himself? Try as he might, Arthur only felt weary. He had already said his good byes in his mind. Was there any other way? Nothing lasted forever. He thanked Gabby for the bike and went on his way.

Chapter 7

Isolated

Ominous. This big, ugly truck parked in front of the adobe scared Arthur. He had heard Juan telling Mary to put their belongings into it. Where would this vehicle take them? Arthur knew anything was possible, and time had taught him a lesson, it could always be worse... Slowly, but surely, the adobe was emptied, along with the few sweet memories they had created. All of it washed away, as if it never existed. One by one, they piled into the truck, inside and out. It was to crowded and Juan made Vivian and Joey get out of the truck. He squeezes his eyes closed, wishing to be as far away as possible. What would happen to them? Maybe they're the lucky ones. As they drive away, his eyes brim sadness and his hands shake waving good bye to them. Was he good to them? Kind? Thoughtful? Arthur has no time for regrets, he squeezes his eyes tighter, shutting out the noise in his head.

They have arrived. How long had they been traveling? It felt like hours, but common sense told him it couldn't have been that long...Arthur wished he had paid attention, instead of curled up in the back of the truck. He watches Juan go into some store, talk to a man and leave some money. As they continue to drive, he looks around and sees nothing but shacks and dirt. Isolated. Ugly. Dirt. This is the new place he chose to move them to?...Arthur's heart is racing, he's scared. Why? He realizes it's all to familiar, hauntingly familiar, except he knows he's not back in Juarez, Mexico. The truck stops on Santa Rosa Street.

Juan gets out of the truck without a word. They all know to do the same. Connie smiles at Arthur as he jumps out and wipes the dirt off his knees. He watches his momma look around...knowing her thoughts. Where exactly are they setting up camp? She grabs the younger girls from the truck while the older ones gather their bags. Arthur and Connie carry the heavier items and follow the caravan down the dirt road. Looming in front of them is this big building. Or is it a church? Arthur isn't sure, but he knows it's not a home. Juan walks through a warehouse door and motions them in. Silently, they file in. Juan gives instructions to Mary and Connie before he leaves. His momma is frustrated and shows it. She walks away, needing to be alone.

Connie gathered the kids together and let them know that this was their new home--abandoned army barracks. It is located near several ranchers and there will be plenty of work. The older girls moaned, not quite accepting it--the younger ones were already exploring and Arthur got to work. He set up each of their sleeping quarters, putting blankets, sleeping bags and pillows in different spots. Arthur pointed out to his unhappy, older sisters that at least there was a roof and a floor. He thought it funny, how quickly they forgot how bad it could be. Grateful, for small measures. His internal clock was ticking, timing was everything concerning Juan. Arthur better have food to feed the girls, Connie and Mary before he returned.

The town looked deserted. Arthur couldn't read the posted signs. He was really disappointed that he didn't grasp the whole concept of reading. "I knew school wasn't an option anymore, so I figured I would just have to teach myself someday." He found a store and asked the man inside where he was--Arvin, California. This was his new hometown. The kind man asked if they were here looking for work. Arthur told him yes, but he saw no fields. He walked the dirt path, following directions, looking for fields or orchards anywhere.

Finally, the beautiful green pastures beckoned him. Arthur ran to the fields and jumped around. He laid down on his back and studied the sky...he could hear birds chirping and saw butterflies floating through the air...here, time was his friend. No rushing, panting, fear...this is where he always finds his peace. Closing his eyes, he wishes he could stay--melding into the earth. It is calm and safe. He knows what to expect in this solitude. A cooing sound gets his attention and he looks around. There, staring back at him, is a small, white dove. Unafraid and injured, it hobbles toward him. Arthur's heart melts and he reaches for the dove. He knows this bird has no one to love, feed, or care for it. Where is his family? Did they abandon him because he was injured? Does that make him worthless? Forgetting about the food he set out to find, he gently wrapped the dove in his shirt and raced back to the army barracks. He felt desperate and exhilarated to save this bird. Did he see himself in this dove? All Arthur wanted was to find Grandma Concha knowing she'd understand.

He ran right into her. She was around the corner from their home. Grandma Concha(Connie) laughed nervously asking where he'd been. She reprimanded him, reminding him that Juan would be furious. He could not just disappear for hours. Ever. Hours? Arthur thought he was only gone for a short time. Time is relentless, raging on. A respecter of no one. The corners of Arthur's mouth turned white with fear looking for Juan. The joy of his dove all but forgotten. It cooed. Connie looked surprised and

Arthur smiled. He asked, "where is he?" She said, "don't worry mijo, he's not back and I found food. Than I went looking for you." He excitedly showed his dove to Connie. She knew, without any words, and walked to the back of the barracks. They were built up on platforms-leaving lots of space below. Underneath the second set of barracks was this large, perfect hiding spot. This would become Arthur's secret haven for the next four years. He quickly and quietly built a little home out of sticks and rocks. His heart stirred with the thoughts of loving and raising this dove. It belonged to him. It renewed something in Arthur. He was hungry for life.

Arthur was learning from his new friend--the dove. He looked forward to spending time with it every day. He'd watch it struggle to move its' broken wing. Life was fragile for this dove, yet he fought valiantly to move. Arthur admired his dove. He decided he'd fight the same way for life. The dove would bravely hop up to him for bread crumbs. It felt good to be wanted and useful. Arthur would treat life with more respect and gratitude, due to his dove. He would not let Juan be in control of his thoughts, no matter what. This would prove to be insurmountable at times for Arthur.

Fear. It is a demon that cripples Arthur, holding him down, slowly suffocating all his good intentions. Juan barrels through their lives with the speed of a revolving cylinder, wreaking havoc and chaos. Arthur is trying to find a balance, a steady hold onto anything. They are all settled in this new town, ready to do his bidding. Living in the barracks is isolating. There is a lot of open space and no one seems to interact with one another anymore. Work is not as easy to come by here. There are plenty of workers available, grown men, and that is who the ranchers want tending their fields. This does not sit well with Juan. Arthur gets his first beating in Arvin. He makes himself heard, loud and clear. Juan quietly and crazily tells his son, "get work, we need food." Arthur feels it coming, in the pit of his stomach, almost making him sick. Fear. His pulse quickening wildly. The moment is overwhelming. He has to quiet it before he loses his mind to it. He breathes deep and the torrent passes. Today, Arthur can and will face the obstacles Juan puts before him.

In no time at all, Arthur has secured some work. He walks to the fields with his older sisters. He is noticing the two oldest girls acting strange. They seem more interested in the guys than working hard and fast. Mary senses it too. She does warn the girls to settle and get to work. Thoughts are swarming through Mary's mind, forcing her to think. How will she keep the girls away from boys? How will Juan react? These things scare her. Life is hard enough. She fears treading new waters with Juan. Mary vaguely remembers life before age eight, but she desperately wants to go back to it. Guilt. It weighs her down, burying her deeper and deeper...he is only eight. Nevertheless, Mary tells Arthur, "protect your sisters please." He hears the pleading in her tone. This young child counts the moments until he can feed his dove.

Chapter 8

The Gap Widens

Arthur hates how he feels, so disconnected from his momma... He strives to please her. It isn't for the same reasons as Juan. Her weariness, heavy heart and lifeless face keep Arthur awake at night. Is he supposed to make it better for her? How? Doesn't she know how hard he tries? He isn't sure how to drudge up more work for all of them. As if on cue, or Arthur wonders if Juan can read his thoughts, he tells them to get into the back of the truck. They are going to find more work. Arthur understands they are of some use to Juan and it feels good. His father won't get rid of him yet. It's a sad thought to Arthur. First, that this man is actually his father, and worse than that, Juan would abandon him if he could. He is determined to never let this happen. Why? He doesn't have an answer. Misery is all he's ever known. He chooses this wretchedness over loneliness. Arthur will work harder than ever.

Juan is many things. He is a man who would do whatever it takes to get what he wants. He wasn't loving or kind, but he could manipulate most people to his advantage. Juan would pack the kids in the back of the truck and put Mary in the front seat right next to him. Loving husband and father...They were instructed to smile and be silent. He started showing up to the different farms and talking to the ranchers. The loving, doting, hard-working husband and father looking for work. These men would soften as soon as they saw all his children. Before long, Juan's family was back to working full time. Timing was perfect because the family was changing.

They all lived together in the barracks. They all worked together in the fields. Yet, Arthur said they had never felt further apart. Maybe it was the disappointment of leaving Edison Highway and their adobe. Maybe everyone was tired and looking for their own way out. Grandma Concha had been rather quiet and more worried than usual. Arthur felt a little invisible to her. It hurt more than he cared to admit. His momma was edgier, angrier and sadder than he could remember. Were they all finally broken? Damaged beyond hope? Something was amiss in this fractured family.

Arthur went straight to his dove after work. There it sat, smiling, at least he thought so. His reliable friend. The broken wing had healed and it saddened Arthur. Does he keep it captive? Or set it free to live it's own life? It was to much to think about right now...and he could hear voices...Arthur walked around the front to the barracks. Joey and Vivian were standing outside looking uneasy. He ran up to them and gave them hugs. Than he heard the shouting--Juan yelling, Mary screaming and Connie crying. He looked at Joey with a million unspoken questions. Grandma Concha walked out than and hugged her two children. Her face soaked with tears, she moaned in half English, half Spanish, "mi ninos-I'm sorry.." The three stood hugging, shutting out the world. Arthur watched quietly. He yearned to be part of their world. Grandma Concha looked up and put out her arms, enveloping him into their circle. Warm tears covered his face.

There were so many questions. All the kids were outside waiting. Grandma Concha(Connie) gently told them that their momma was going to be having another baby. She asked them to stay out of the barracks because Juan was upset. Is that why he was calling his momma a whore? Is that why he beat her up? Arthur didn't realize that Juan was accusing her of sleeping with other men...he also had no idea that his momma didn't want Vivian and Joey around. It caused friction between Mary and Connie. Juan didn't care. He told them to figure it out and settle it. Arthur was somber, feeling heavy for his mom and this baby. Would it be a girl? Or another boy that Juan could beat up? Another mouth to feed...when does it end? He ran to the back, grabbed his dove and took off. He found his spot in the fields and sat. The dove was cooing and relaxed. It had grown to trust Arthur. Tears streaming down his face, he kissed his dove and said good bye. He felt a presence and turned around. Penny, one of his sisters, ran up to him and soothed him. He opened up to the warmth of her hug. Arthur told her to lay down in the pastures and look up. He decided to share his special place with her...

Together they listen to the cooing of the doves. He is teaching her how to find peace here. She must pay attention to the details. He says it's like paying tribute to nature. Arthur shows her the reeds growing free and wild in the fields. He wishes to be one. Penny giggles and enjoys their alone time. She promises not to tell anyone about his secret place or his doves. Much to his delight, Arthur has found three more injured doves. Penny struggles to keep up as he races back to the barracks. She's wondering what he's going to do with these little creatures, following him to this deserted spot behind their home. He silently scoots them into this little nest like cage, spreads out bread crumbs and leaves water. She watches in awe. He did it all so quickly...Did he build the cage? Will he heal the doves? Penny trusts Arthur completely. She wants to hang out there and watch the doves heal. He's agitated now though, and seems to be in a hurry. She asks, "what's wrong mijo?" Arthur is astonished she'd ask. He doesn't answer, but runs around the corner, hoping Juan isn't home yet...

He catches Grandma Concha's look and knows it's to late. Arthur motions to Penny to back away. She's 10 months older but small, and the thought of her getting slapped around hurts him. Juan doesn't say a word and Arthur assumes the position. The quicker he moves and obeys, the better. He stiffens his scarred, skinny frame waiting for pain to overtake his back. Juan yells at him every time he beats him with the whip..."cavron(bastard), perezoso(lazy), ladino(sneaky)... Where do you go?

And why take your sister?" Arthur knows better than to answer. Crying is out of the question, but tears cover his face. This angers Juan even more and he tells him to be a man. Juan looks at Mary-she's holding her swollen belly-and shakes his head. He tells her to keep the girls away from Arthur and he leaves. Only than, does the household take a breath. Cries are softly heard and Connie wipes the splatter of blood off the floor and wall. Arthur gingerly walks outside and hoses off his welted, bloodied back. Penny is trying to be brave, but can't hold back her tears as she wraps a towel around him...he comforts her with a feeble smile.

Arthur makes sure Juan has left and goes back to his doves. He feeds them, holds them and loves them. He decides than that he will raise an entire family of animals. Though the sun is setting, he is on the hunt for wire, sticks and nails. Arthur realizes he will need a big cage for the family he will have soon. He can't wait to share this with Grandma Concha(Connie). He's racing back to her again. The excitement on his face lightens her heart. His eyes are dancing as he tells her the grand plan. She smiles at the wonderment of his childlike enthusiasm. She wants to wrap him in her arms and protect him forever. Instead, she promises to help him starting tomorrow. As he is changing and getting ready for bed, she notices one of the welts on his back is opened and bloody. When his breathing has slowed and the room has quieted with everyone drifting to sleep, she gently wipes his gash. Through her tears, she begs god to give this little boy a chance to become a young man. She stays on her knees praying for protection.

Morning comes soon. The sunlight streaming through the barracks promises a new day. Chaos has taken over and kids are everywhere. Somehow, Juan decided to let the younger girls go to school and have Connie stay home watching the toddlers. Arthur is envious and hoping he gets the opportunity to go back to school again. For now, he and his five older sisters go off to work. He races to check on his doves and than catches up with the girls. Arthur wonders why his momma was no where to be seen. After a long day of picking onions, cutting off the stems and bagging them, he would come home to a surprise.

Juan was standing at the door with his arms folded across his chest-expressionless. Arthur wondered why...His heart was racing, his steps slowing, and fear gripping his mind. His little sisters, Lita and Cristina, ran up to the six of them exclaiming, "Momma had baby Elaina--come look." The look on Juan's face changed. The girls walked in, but Arthur knew better. He thought of his new sister as he was walking to his doves, and felt indifferent. Only his little creatures could stir his emotions. Well, not quite, Juan's presence stirred many emotions. As he was kneeling on the dirt, his doves hopped all around him. He knew they liked him. This gave Arthur great joy.

Time passed quickly and quietly. Seasons came and went. His sisters got older. They seemed to work less and less, but he didn't know why. He had a feeling it had something to do with the guys he'd watch hanging around the fields. As long as Juan wasn't angry, he didn't mind much. Arthur never took the calm for granted. He slipped in and out of his home as stealthily as possible. His menagerie of animals continued to grow. There were 20 to 30 doves at any given time. He was fascinated by these creatures. As they started laying "miniature eggs," he was so excited that he'd drag grandma Concha to the site. She was always taken aback by his gentle love for anything, so grateful he wasn't bitter or loveless. She would do anything to nourish his innocence and love for life.

Grandma Concha goes to great lengths to spend time with Arthur. These two steal away and spend carefree, unforgettable moments. They will be etched in Arthur's heart forever. Memories of her taking the time to show her love for him still bring tears to his eyes. Many moments are spent with the doves. She teaches Arthur how to feed them oats in order to strengthen them. Than, much to his delight, grandma cooks the mini eggs and serves Arthur. She would treat him like a prince and they'd laugh. Simple pleasures. He says, "it would be the only time in my life I'd feel special, until I would meet my wife and children." Connie, unknowingly, created a ray of hope in an otherwise bleak life.

Time spent with Grandma Concha(Connie) always energized Arthur. His mind would be his saving grace. Arthur never stops planning, plotting, thinking...He decided to plant a garden. Grabbing the seeds was the easy part. He took them from every field his hands worked, and than gently wrapped them in toilet paper. His eyes scanned the area, wondering where he could hide his garden from Juan. Something so simple and innocent as a field of veggies and fruit, would end in a horrible beating if his father discovered it. Arthur knew that Juan couldn't stand him to experience any form of happiness. Nor would he ever allow it. Why? All Arthur ever wanted to know was why?....the unanswered question plagues him to this day.

Chapter 9

Secret Haven

A blessing and a curse, Arthur buried his thoughts and moved forward. His garden was flourishing and the sight of it brought such pleasure. Much to his delight, one by one, jack rabbits started hanging out in his garden. Within hours, Arthur found more wire and built a very large cage. As usual, these little critters took to him. Arthur would sit motionless, as the rabbits would hop up and sit next to his feet. The sight of their twitching, pink noses always drew a laugh from him. There was a bond formed and these rabbits would hop into the cage and stay. Arthur was very pleased. The only people he shared his passion with were Grandma Concha(Connie) and his sister Penny. He knew they understood. His grandma loved to see him smile.

Life was difficult. It wasn't just the physical labor that exhausted Arthur, it was the mental game he had to play to keep afloat. He had accepted that he was unwanted and worthless. He accepted the daily beatings. He even accepted being hungry, cold and dirty. He succumbed to his lot in life without complaining. But the mental anguish that Juan loved causing Arthur hurt. There were days that he felt that he wouldn't make it. By age nine, Arthur was a weary, old soul. Grandma Concha(Connie) understood this. It gave her great joy to love him any chance she could. Since they weren't allowed to openly show love to one another, she'd look for any way possible. With tears running down her face, the words came tumbling out, as Connie smiled and said, "Juan is letting you go to school! You must still work though." Arthur wasn't certain that he heard her correctly, but he threw his arms around her and smiled.

Being a child still, he took off running to his little paradise. He laid right in the middle of it. His garden on one side, his rabbits on the other and the beautiful, endless sky above him. He opened the cage and his friends hopped all around him. Arthur thanked anyone listening. For a moment, he believed life to be perfect. Time was a rarity for him. There was no time for moments like this, really. His adrenaline at high speed, he put away his bunnies and raced home. He knew Juan must be around because it was a silent house. Everyone moved around like a corpse. His food was on the steps--hidden. Arthur grabbed the bowl and slurped up his soup in seconds. He quietly left it hidden where he found it, and walked into the kitchen.

Juan glared at him. Smiling eerily he said, "cavron, there will be another baby." Arthur knew better, but he was confused and spoke. "What do you mean?" His answer was a violent strike to his son's face. The gasps were barely audible...though the family was used to the cruelty from this man, it still took their breath away. Arthur walked out as quietly as he'd walked in, barely feeling the sting and unaware of the swelling on the right side of his face. His thoughts were on this child-another one...emotions out of control. He would put his focus on school. Arthur curled up under the barracks, let his bunnies out for warmth and was so grateful to be away from him.

Juan was in a mood that shut the house down immediately. It was early evening still, dinner interrupted, dishes everywhere and upset children. Juan gave no one a thought beyond himself. Mary shut off lights and everyone knew not to question or complain. Grandma Concha(connie) wiped away her silent tears and prayed that her little guy was safe and warm. She knew he would not be allowed back in the house tonight.

The rising of the sun was always a welcome sight. Arthur loved the way it warmed his bones. A new day, new beginnings, a fresh start...all of it kept him hopeful. The mind, such a powerful, incredible mechanism. He happily fed all his bunnies and put them away. Arthur entered the barracks trepidatiously. The peaceful quiet hiding the reality of what went on behind closed doors. Grandma Concha(Connie) was already up cleaning and making lunches for the younger kids. She smiled as she heard him creep in. He had time to brush his teeth and run to the fields. As she watched him running, matted hair, yesterday's clothes and probably hungry, she closed her eyes and prayed again. It was a rare moment when Connie was worry free. It lightened her heart to hear him whistling, as if he didn't have a problem in the world. At times like this, she'd find herself dreaming about the five children she was forced to abandon. The jolt to her heart would leave her breathless, holding the counter to steady herself, she'd take a deep breath and push the hysteria rising up within her down deep.

Arthur watches his sisters working in unison, feeling conflicted about many things. He studies them individually and is certain he's failed them, though if you asked him, he wouldn't know how to change their lives. So much was expected of them. The work was toiling and nonstop. He felt it was to much for them because they were girls. They were not able to keep up with the him, the other men or Juan's expectations. As soon as he was done with his rows, he'd move to theirs. Arthur would pick their rows of cotton quickly, while they rested. It gave him peace of mind. After a long, arduous day, Arthur would start the walk home alone. Juan had already picked up the girls, as usual, with no regard to his son. Arthur figured it was just as well, no one could hurt him when he was alone, not physically anyway. The emotional toll would shatter his soul into many pieces, over and over again, until he was a splintered boy.

Nature... something about it was soothing to his mind and broken heart. It felt like a healing ointment being poured over an open wound. It drowned out the words, "you will never amount to anything," "you are worthless".....it all faded away. Arthur is happy to be lost in the outdoors. Nothing escapes him-- birds chirping, the ground crunching under his steps, and butterflies floating past him. He draws in deep breaths, hungry to be free from his life. His feet are moving faster and faster. When he focuses, Arthur realizes he's standing in front of the small school. His excitement cannot be contained and he jumps in the air. This will be his school. He cannot wait to meet his new teacher, wondering if she will like him...he takes off running again, by the time he looks up he's back at the barracks. Arthur hopes Grandma Concha(Connie) is around.

She is on her hands and knees, always cleaning. The sound of his footsteps draws her attention. As Grandma Concha looks up, she wipes her tears. Her mouth is bloody. Arthur's anger starts to surface and he can't contain it. He glares at her and walks out silently. She tries to stop him, "mijo, esta buen," but he's gone. Arthur is running, while kicking the ground silently. He comes upon a tree far enough from the barracks, and screams. He beats his fists into the tree trunk, until they are bloody and he's breathless. He falls to his knees, covering his face. Deep sobs wracking his crumpled, boyish body. The hatred for this man runs deep. It rages through his mind like a fierce wildfire. His thoughts make him feel guilty. He walks back slowly to his hidden oasis. The garden of veggies and the smell of his bunnies draw his mind to a peaceful place. As easily as flipping a light switch off and on, he shuts out his thoughts. After cleaning up his wounds, he heads back to his house for a fresh start.

Grandma Concha was prepared. She put on her best smile, as easily as if she were putting on her Sunday bests. They each had a role to play in this house of horrors, veering away from it could cause the fragile house to cave in. They clung to what they knew for survival. He softened at her warm smile, choosing to believe it was genuine and no longer saw the battered face. Arthur's hug couldn't conceal the desperateness they both felt or the atrocities they faced daily, yet he cherished the simple touch of her hands. Sometimes he believed she could read his mind. Grandma Concha said, "your momma says you will start school tomorrow. I will have your lunch packed. Don't forget it on your way to work." He should've been excited, but his attention was focused on his momma who walked in. Her ever growing belly upset him. She stared back at her little boy, taken aback by the changes in him. He was growing up and she hadn't noticed. Mary walked up to him and gently caressed his bruised face.

Tears don't come easily for Arthur, but the yearning for love and the gentle touch from his momma break him down. He reaches out and holds her hand tightly, drawing in a deep breath. The facade crumbles and the tears spill forth, like a well sprouting a leak. Arthur doesn't care. He is grateful for this simple moment. Emotions, such a frightful display of reality, causes both of his 'momma's' to turn away leaving him alone in his thoughts.

A penny for his thoughts...Arthur says he can't remember what he was thinking that day, all he knows is he allowed his thoughts to consume him. With no regard to Juan, he walked aimlessly to his haven. The sound of heavy breathing caused the hair on his skin to stand up. Juan grabbed his shoulder with such intensity, Arthur winced against his will. "Where do you go?," he screamed in his face. Arthur couldn't speak for many reasons. His fear of Juan paralyzed him from head to toe, and no one, not even Juan would take away his hidden Havana. He knew what was coming next. It wouldn't last long. One blow to his face knocks him to the ground. The kicks come and go without much pain. It is over. Arthur rolls over and sits up when it's safe. He smiles knowing that Juan left frustrated. It's the pain Juan wants to see, and Arthur is determined not to give him that. His stubbornness, which he is known for, plays in his favor.

Arthur refuses to go home, after that beating, no matter that it's cold or that's he hungry. He took off walking. In his anger, he hopes that they all worry about him, as he arrives back at the barracks. Settling in for the night in his hidden spot, the sight of his many bunnies keep his spirit light. He misses the doves and their cooing sounds, and wonders why he never sees them around anymore. Arthur's attitude is poor and it makes him angrier. The thought of Juan controlling everything, even his thoughts, scares him. "I knew if I let myself slip into that dark hole of anger and vengeance, I'd never come out of it. The older I was getting, the harder it was becoming to control my rage. I looked for a new outlet. I would not become like him," Arthur said.

He pulled out his shiny new marbles and smiled. Arthur acquired them while on his walk. He couldn't wait to show the kids at school tomorrow. Arthur didn't feel so good about stealing them, but he consoled himself trying to believe he earned them. Arthur was ambitious and always looking for ways to eat, earn hidden money and trinkets. Owning anything, even junk, helped him to not feel so worthless. The words pounded into his head day and night were hard to overcome, but he never gives up the battle. This is how he justifies stealing the marbles from the kind lady. His mind never resting, he watches her hauling wood and knows it's a way to earn some kind of treat. Arthur asks if he can help and she is grateful. As he is putting the wood in her little shop, his eyes light up with all the treasures in there. The steely marbles stand out and Arthur is mesmerized by them. He's never owned new ones. His marbles are from the trash, old and dingy. He grabs a packet of the marbles and runs as fast as his feet will go. Unaware, the sweet, old woman waves good bye, thanking him. Sitting under the barracks, oblivious to the dried blood from his earlier beating covered in dirt, staining his skin, Arthur gives thanks for his newfound treasure.

Exhaustion takes over. He wakes up startled, spilling his marbles all over. Arthur hurriedly puts his bunnies in their cage. He stops and stares at them, realizing they are overcrowded. When did they become so many?... He laughs at his thoughts, comparing them to his momma- "Don't worry-we are to many also...I will build you a bigger cage." Running to the front of the barracks shivering, he pleads out loud- "please be up momma concha." Only the moon appears to be awake, shining bright in the sky. Arthur knows it matters what he wears to school. Kids can be mean. Grandma is waiting with his clothes, mended and clean, and his lunch bag. He dips the cloth into a cold bucket of water and scrubs off the blood and dirt. He runs to the fields, passing his older sisters and momma yelling, "race you!" His excitement for school can't be contained. It puts a smile on their faces. Arthur has no idea that he is an inspiration to them all. They know if he can fight this hard to live, so can they.

Chapter 10

His Moment

One thing all people will agree on that have ever met Arthur, he's never met a stranger. First day of school for him, went by without a hitch. School had been in session for several months, and everyone had already formed their circle of friends, but Arthur mixed in with everyone. He eagerly shared his steely marbles and showed off his skills. Of course, he had spent many hours practicing on his old set of marbles so that he could be the best. He was not so confident when it came to schoolwork. It was not from lack of trying, he was just to far behind. His teacher, Ms. Ganet, had a soft spot for this youngster immediately. She watched him come and go on foot, by himself and tried getting background information. As usual, he was tightlipped. Arthur did anything he could to please her though. He'd wipe down the chalkboard, respect all her rules and study hard in class.

Ms. Ganet worked endlessly with Arthur, nevertheless, he wasn't progressing in the classroom. Outside the class was another story altogether. She could hear cheering on the playground and walked outside to observe the happenings. There he was in the center of the circle, teaching all the kids how to play marbles. It became the talk of the school and soon enough, kids wanted to challenge him. Arthur thought this was the greatest achievement he'd ever accomplished. For a short while, he could be just a kid, lost in the game of marbles. Arthur and steely marbles became synonymous.

These few months of attending school, put an urgency to learn all he could, deep within his spirit. Arthur had always worked hard at anything he did. Prior to this though, it was laced with fear. This was entirely different. For the first time in his life, he experienced a sense of accomplishment and he loved it. Arthur was going to be the best at marbles and try harder at schoolwork. Friends would know it and like him for it. When he realized that schoolwork was going to be an issue, a solution was found. Arthur told his Grandma Concha that he had to wear long sleeved shirts to school from now on.

Always eager to see him happy, Connie didn't question him. Underneath those sleeves, Arthur would write down all the questions and answers for each days homework. He did not fail. This went on for the remainder of his school experience. Who knows if Ms. Ganet was aware of this, she never said a word. She only had kind words and a big smile for Arthur.

He continued to work long hard hours in the fields. The abuse, the beatings, the cruelty, inflicted by Juan also didn't change. But Arthur had become quite adept at shutting him out, refusing to let Juan devour him like a deadly cancer. Instead, his thoughts were consumed with marbles and school. Ms. Ganet had told Arthur about an inter-school contest for the best marble player. His mind was made up. He would beat out everyone in his school, so he could travel to the other campus to compete. Arthur said, "I had never been so excited about anything like this in my life." This 10-year-old boy had something to reach for, and it kept him grounded in his ever changing, unstable existence.

In the midst of fieldwork, schooling, marble practice, tending to his garden and bunnies, as well as keeping food on the table, Arthur is still aware of the changing in the air. Something is amiss. It's like a weight in the pit of his stomach, causing him to walk slower and focus on his surroundings. What is he looking for? He isn't sure. There aren't many things he is sure of with so much uncertainty ruling his daily life. He checks off a mental list of what he does know—work, hunger, school, marbles, Juan—he is still puzzled by what he senses but can't see. So, in spite of his life, he reacts like a typical 10-year-old and gets lost in his world of marbles.

A few weeks have flown by and Arthur has won every marble tournament the schools have put on in Arvin. His family is unaware of any of this. He races home excited to share the news, until he arrives there. The weight of the tension and fear at this house overwhelm him, dissipating any excitement. Suddenly, marbles-competitions and school all seem so silly…maybe even selfish. He questions himself, feeling bad that he gets to escape every day for a few hours. Guilt takes over. It makes Arthur sad and more lonely than usual. Trudging over to his hideaway, he allows his bunnies to console him, with the warmth of the sun peeking in, relaxing his body.

Arthur loves the changing of seasons. He doesn't know the month or which day of the week it is- though Ms. Ganet is working endlessly on this with him. He only knows the warmth is coming and is ready for it. It's been a brutal winter, leaving his hands raw and callous from the early morning frost. His feet fare no better. Until he went to school, and Ms. Ganet gave him a pair of warm shoes, he'd go to work barefoot or with ripped shoes. Grandma Concha tried to make sure he always had footwear, whether she sewed something together for him, or found used shoes somewhere. But it was difficult to keep up with a growing boy. He'd never noticed his hands before, until a kid at school asked him why they looked funny. Arthur didn't respond, he just blocked it out, as he would continue to do whenever it was a painful subject. His rough worn-out hands, would one day be treasured by his own family.

His mind drifted to the big competition coming up. Arthur was Arvin Elementary school's star marble player. They were going to drive him to Bakersfield in the big school bus. His reddish-brown eyes lit up with excitement at the thought of it. How would he pull this off? Could Grandma Concha cover for him without a beating? He would be gone all day, missing the morning/afternoon cotton-picking job that his family counted on. He hoped that Juan would disappear, as he often did. Arthur finally confided in his grandma and sister Penny. Both of them were nervous, but Grandma Concha told him to go. She would figure it out. As it turned out, in the middle of the night, his momma went into labor, giving birth to another baby girl--Maria. The whole house was up for the entire night because Mary had her babies there. The kids would run back and forth, mainly Arthur, bringing fresh buckets of water for the delivery. Grandma Concha would tear up sheets to make blankets and Mary would lay there, silently, while bringing another child into her very cruel world. Though Arthur was exhausted, the birth of his baby sister worked in his favor. For a day or two, the arrival of a new life brought with it, a certain kind of gentleness to their home. Grandma Concha looked how she felt, worn out and much older than her years. But she smiled at him. That smile always warmed him up inside.

He slipped out quietly, after giving his new sister a kiss on the forehead. Arthur ran as fast as his skinny legs could move, fearful he'd miss the bus. The anticipation of the competition had him bouncing up and down on his seat. Ms. Ganet smiled at him and told him it would be a fun day-no matter who won. It was surreal…a dream come true. Arthur was in awe looking at the scenery as they drove to Bakersfield. He thought it was beautiful. They finally arrived at BHS--Bakersfield High School. The games began. Arthur had more fun than he knew possible. He made it to the final round but lost to a boy two years older than him. It didn't faze him though. His eyes were fixated on the second place trophy. Both boys were brought up to the podium at the front of the auditorium. Everyone was standing up-clapping and cheering. Arthur said, "walking to the front was magical and I didn't know I was crying until Ms. Ganet wiped my cheeks. Her eyes were also watering as she handed me my trophy." The principal than took their pictures. Arthur watched all the happenings around him, not able to fully comprehend that this was all for him. It was unreal. He hugged the trophy tightly on the drive back, his scarred knuckles turning white from his grip. Arthur was so happy, so proud and so sad that it was over. He wondered how he was going to protect his trophy from Juan. Lost in his thoughts, Arthur was unaware that Ms. Ganet was watching him.

All the students and teachers of Arvin elementary were in the parking lot when the bus pulled in. There were balloons and congratulations signs streaming across the foyer. Arthur's mouth was wide open, eyes huge and palms moist from excitement. He could not believe what he was seeing. Try as he might, he could not celebrate like everyone else. He was so lost, always on the brink of losing his mind, he didn't know how to let go and revel in the moment. He followed his teacher into the auditorium where Arthur was given a ribbon and small trophy with his name on it. Than Ms. Ganet walked him to the main corridor of the school, opened a hutch filled with many trophies, and placed his large one alongside the others. Above the trophy sits a picture of him. Arthur wonders where she got that picture. She is beaming and explaining that scrolled above the picture it says,

"Arthur Rodriguez-2nd Place Champion." The school day ends much like it started, surreal. Arthur walks home, mini trophy in hand, slowly. He wants to absorb it all. These were the best few months of his life. Juan could never take it away. When Arthur talks about it today, his eyes still light up at the sweet memory of it all. It would be the last time he sees Ms. Ganet, or is allowed to return to school…for a very long time.

Chapter 11

Changes

Juan had heard something about the steely marble contest. Though he kicked, punched and bullied Arthur about it, his lips were sealed. Arthur would rather take the beating than let this man he despised destroy his last few special months. Juan was angry. He was crueler than usual and around far to often. He would seek Arthur out and kick him around for any reason, or no reason at all. After 15-hour workdays, Arthur could expect a beating because Juan felt the girls worked to slow, or the barracks were dirty, or Donna was missing again. Juan coughed all the time now. Arthur thought something was wrong with him. He appeared shaky and thinner. Juan would yell at Grandma Concha(connie) and his momma to "fix him up."

They'd scramble around, like lost children, trying to please him. He'd slap one, than the other. Arthur watched them heat up honey and whiskey. This would calm Juan for a while. Arthur would have such rage take over his mind, he'd run blindly until he'd find a tree, beating it every time until hands were raw and bloody. He says, "the only thing I saw every time I punched the tree was Juan's face." Arthur knew Juan was losing control of his older sisters and it was making him crazier.

Donna, known as Lola, is Arthur's oldest sister. He viewed her more as a "momma" figure. She was, after all, only 12 years younger than his mom Mary. Lola also kept very much to herself, just like his mom. Donna is beautiful, with her green eyes and long black hair. She is feisty and not afraid to fight with Juan anymore. This shocks Arthur, but it seems to have worked. Other than showing up for work, she does her own thing…coming and going as she pleases. Even though Arthur is punished for this, he is genuinely happy for her. It gives him a glimmer of hope, that they might all have the chance to live outside the prison walls that bind them, physically anyway. Would he ever escape from the prison walls of his mind? It is getting harder to contain his anger. Arthur knows he needs to keep busy physically, but without school, marble

competitions or Ms. Ganet, picking cotton isn't enough. He is resilient, determined and a fighter. Arthur just has to remind himself of this. He walks to the open orchards, the one place he can relax his mind and gain control of his thoughts, but his pace is slow and painful. Each step is a reminder of how much his 10-year-old body has already endured.

There won't be peace for his mind on this afternoon.

Scattered thoughts, nothing making sense… Arthur wants to leave, disappear into the orchards like his doves, untangle himself from the strangling arms of

his family. Guilt won't allow him to bolt. Fear will keep him paralyzed. Anger, it can work for you or against you, Arthur chooses to let his anger propel him forward. He will go home, take care of his family and find a new beginning.

Arthur somehow found the courage to ask Juan if he could come home later, after the fieldwork was done. He quickly went on to explain that he was looking for extra work. Juan was very distracted lately, today was no exception. He told Arthur to move closer to him when he spoke. Arthur inched up closer and closer, eyes half shut, hoping to dull the pain the inevitable blow would bring across his face. He didn't expect the fierce pain shooting down his check to his neck. He opened his eyes at the sound of Juan's deep, cruel chuckle. As Arthur was covering his nose to slow the blood from pouring out, Juan told him, "do what you want cavron, but your work better be done. Don't make me find you." Arthur stood there alone, shaking, unsure of what happened. He wasn't aware that he was crying out loud. The pain was sharper than he ever remembered before. Grandma Concha had ears everywhere, and gasped when she saw him. She started to cry as she gently pressed cold, wet rags to his face. She asked him, "why mijo? Why?" Arthur had no answer, nor was she expecting one. As she was cleaning the blood from his forehead and eyes, he realized Juan had slammed his face into that broken glass table. Shattered glass was everywhere. His eyes were swelling closed quickly and grandma explained that his nose was broken.

Arthur was sure he'd never heard his sweet Grandma Concha cry with such emotion. That hurt him more than his face. Connie kept muttering, "this is because of lola, not you, because of lola…" he didn't ask what she meant. He didn't care.

The next morning, his bruised face, swollen eyes and cut lip quieted everyone in the house, and anyone who saw him in the fields. Arthur worked fast and furious, without thoughts or emotion. He said he vaguely remembered the day go by. On the way home from work, he saw his momma throwing up by the barracks and felt disgusted. He wanted to be concerned, but his anger was stronger. Instead, he went to his hidden oasis, laid down and slept.

Awakened by someone shaking him, he jumped. Penny was staring at him intently. "What!" he asked, "what is it?" She told him, "Lola is getting married, momma and grandma are planning the wedding and Juan is letting her!" Things made sense now. Arthur knew why his face was slammed into a table. Changes…he had lost his grip on lola. Arthur knew it must be Jake that she'd marry. He'd watch them hang out a lot and leave together. Juan was right about this, Arthur didn't try to stop it. He was glad. All he could think to say was "run Lola, as fast as you can." As they were walking to the house, Penny casually said, "momma is having another baby." Those words numbed his mind-made him feel sick. For the first time, in quite some time, he wanted to comfort his momma. He walked into the house, looked around for Juan, and than hugged her tightly. Mary didn't react to his embrace, she stiffened under his touch. But Arthur knew what she felt. It caused him to hug her even tighter, wanting her to know she wasn't alone…or was that for himself? She endures the same abuse he does, and more than he cares to imagine. Mary gently removes his embrace and tells him they are planning a wedding for Lola, a happy occasion. Arthur shakes his head acknowledging that he knows. Mary smiles and leaves the rooms. He finds it comforting that she doesn't mention the baby. His momma is like him, always creating her own reality…

Life took on a different attitude for a short time. Did Juan feel defeated, beaten down or was he just tired? He allowed the planning of the wedding to move forward and involved himself in different ways. The mood was lighter throughout the house, Arthur relished every minute of that. He was certain that Juan got involved and put on a happy face, because while he couldn't stop Lola, he'd never admit that to anyone-especially himself. Jake's family, Lola's fiancée, even came around to consult with Connie and Mary about the wedding dress and food. Juan's pride wouldn't allow help from anyone, so he told them he'd handle it all. Of course, Juan was cordial, even friendly. Jake's family was grateful for the kindness. This was a side of Juan his family had never experienced.

It was a whirlwind of an affair, a dress and decorations to be made, menu's to create and a dance to plan. Juan wanted it to look good. Appearances mattered, not reality. Arvin was a small town and he knew it would be talked about. Money would not be an issue. Truth told, there was always plenty of it, the family worked hard. The problem was Juan and his gambling/drinking issues. Not this time. He made sure Connie and Mary had enough money for the event that would show people who he is.

The girls were caught up in the wedding hype, leaving the workload on Arthur's shoulders. Juan even showed up and worked, instead of just barking out orders. Arthur worked fast and furious, but paid attention to Juan interacting with the other men. Who is this man? Arthur wondered how he could be so nice to these strangers--holding conversations, even laughing. As the sound of laughter drifted over from the direction of Juan, he would have to stop and look. This young boy could not remember a time he'd ever heard Juan laugh before. Certainly, he and Juan had never held a conversation. Looking down, Arthur felt a searing sharp pain shoot throughout his body, as if it were crushing him. Yet, there was nothing touching him. He wiped his eyes dry and kept on working--robotic like--alone, empty and cold.

The countdown to the wedding flew on by. The big day was here. It was a nice summer day, excitement and chaos of a different kind filled the Rodriguez home. Arthur liked watching his sisters smile. Grandma Connie and his momma went through the motions, but, try as he might, Arthur didn't see happiness on their faces. The smiles were there, frozen in time, empty eyes, lost souls. He went on to work, hoping to be done in time for the wedding.

The sun was setting, and the church was crowded. Arthur stood in the back and was mesmerized at the beauty of it all. He couldn't take his eyes off of Donna and Jake. It was their gaze at one another that enthralled him. A dream took root in his heart, mind, and soul. He would find a bride that would one day love him with that same look. Arthur knew that he'd know it was her, just by seeing her. A seed of hope was planted on that summer wedding day.

Summer was coming to an end, Donna was moving away and the heaviness in the home was palpable. This family unit depended on each other. They were appendages to one another, their strength in facing abuse and pain was in their numbers. Arthur could hear his momma crying in the barracks, as Donna and Jake drove off to Porterville to start their life. He was envious of her escape and dreamed of his, believing it to be a possibility. Arthur took a deep breath, desperate to keep from slipping into that abyss that surrounds him. He walked into the barracks and put his arms around his momma, comforting her. For the first time, she allowed him to, sinking into his embrace and crying gently. Such a sadness came over Arthur when he realized he only felt responsible for her...no warmth or love for his momma...Why? He wants to feel love for his momma and he needs her love back...time moves on and thoughts of love and his momma fade away, irrelevant, like the life he lives.

Chapter 12

How Many More?

Arthur watches her rub her belly, sweat and dirt running down her neck. Tattered clothes stretched out to the seams by the ever growing bump. He studies her, she is so beautiful. Momma Mary looks exhausted. There may be no love lost between them, but his compassion for her runs deep. He walks over and wipes her face with his shirt, surprised at how tall he is standing next to her. The irony doesn't escape him that he is growing one way and his momma is growing another. Try as he might, Arthur finds it hard to picture his momma not pregnant. Unsettled thoughts clutter his mind... Does she like being pregnant? Does she want another baby? Will it be another girl? Arthur is jealous of her relationship with his sisters. Maybe another boy would cause her to like him...He knows it doesn't matter and walks away angry. Arthur accepts that they are meaningless, good for nothing, not worthwhile, but his anger surges out of control, rendering him helpless against his thoughts.

Self pity is gnawing at his mind and he is afraid of what he feels. All he wants is to hurt Juan just like he hurts them. He hates being manipulated by his emotions. Arthur wonders where Juan has been, as he realizes no one has seen him since the wedding.

It's a blessing that Juan stays away, his outbursts are not as often, but they are much more intense. The last couple of beatings left Arthur with a broken nose, back pain and a twisted ankle. A very strange feeling has settled in his stomach now too. Even if Juan is no where in sight, terror has taken over Arthur. He cannot shake the uneasiness. Anxiety has reared its ugly head and taken root in his core. More and more, Arthur is sleeping under the barracks with his animals. As he lays on his stomach, he draws in the dirt, wondering how old he actually is. Sweet memories of school waft through his mind...Ms. Ganet had celebrated his birthday with a group of kids that had summer birthdays. He thought that was one of the nicest things ever done for him. Anxiety subsiding, sleep finally takes over...

Sun filtering through the slats of the barracks brings a smile to Arthur's sleepy face. Within seconds, he's up and running, fearful he overslept and Juan beat him to the fields. As he's racing past his home, the commotion there stopped him still. His heart racing, he runs into the barracks and was greeted by the arrival of sister #10--Alicia... He was once again mesmerized by the look his momma had on her face as she gazed at this new little girl. Arthur walked up and kissed baby Alicia on the cheek and froze with fear. He knew Juan must be nearby. The booming voice brought him to attention. "Let's go cavron," Juan said. Every eye turned to Arthur in silent horror, as they watched them walk out in complete silence. For the first time ever, Arthur walked to work with Juan...he was surprised how short this man was.

He expected complete silence or a beating...he did not expect a conversation of any kind, much less this one. Juan asked Arthur, "have you been with a whore yet? It's time. Be a man cavron, understand?" He had no answer for Juan. A swift elbow to the side of Arthur's face prompted him to say yes. With that, Arthur was left standing alone near the working fields, unsure of what just happened. As he started working, many memories flooded his mind... Arthur knew far to well what the word 'whore' meant. Visions of his old job swept through his mind...he had forgotten about the hookers, the smoke filled room & the cruelties he and his momma had endured. His stomach started aching at the thought of Juan's words, what meaning do they hold for his life now?...

A strange calm came over Arthur, this wasn't the first time he experienced this feeling and he had no idea what it was, but he liked it. He vowed to hold tight to the comforting presence that surrounded him. It wasn't tangible, yet he knew it was real. In the beginning Arthur would brush aside this warm presence, almost unaware of it. One particular night, as he lay crying under the barracks, Arthur couldn't ignore this assured feeling in his gut. He started noticing, as he got older, anytime hopelessness invaded his mind, this unexplainable comforting presence covered him, head to toe. Arthur believed it must be the angels or god his grandma prayed to. He inhaled it in deeply, feeding his starving soul, wishing to make it last forever.

Time was a funny concept to Arthur. There never seemed to be enough of it, and yet to much, when it came to sleep. It appeared to drag on when he measured it by his dreams and plans to escape. He wondered what his exact age was because he felt this same age forever...minute by minute he could hear the mental clock tick, it made Arthur anxious. His mind never rested anymore. Even the restful sleep he once looked forward to in his little haven, hidden under the barracks-had slowly dissipated...like water on a hot summer day. His fragile strength was becoming apparent to him and it scared him. Arthur wanted to be set free desperately, mentally, and physically. His mind was racing, trying to figure out what to do with the sleeping hours.

He wondered how summer had slipped away and he hadn't noticed...though the weather was cold now-dampness all around Arthur under the barracks-he welcomed it. The crispness in the air was a change-and almost any change was a welcomed distraction from his thoughts. He didn't like that he could plainly see how broken, alone and insignificant he was. The only certainty in his life was to keep busy-it kept his thoughts at bay. Avoiding Juan was no easy task either. Ever since the birth of Alicia-for some unknown reason-he hung around often. Arthur thought maybe he felt the loss of Lola, like they all did. Sometimes Arthur forgot she was gone-other times he missed her terribly. He had heard Grandma Concha and his momma talking about Lola and his half siblings-- Joey & Vivian. Where were they?...

He closed his eyes, drifting off and dreaming about heading to Bakersfield...maybe he'd find Joey and Vivian...maybe not, but he would've escaped Arvin and Juan. This place seemed to be shrinking, his momma, grandma and animals all slipping from his grasp. Anger was taking over all his emotions and nothing seemed to stop it. He was finding it harder and harder to breathe. Juan was always in a foul mood nowadays. It appeared he picked on Elaina too. Anytime he came anywhere near her, she screamed and ran. Arthur didn't understand why or how he could possibly do that. She was just a little girl. The cruelties of this man left Arthur dumbfounded. Somehow he knew Juan had plans for him by the way he kept watching him. It was altogether different from the past. Sleep would evade him this night, but Arthur used the time to draw up a way to make more money to please his father.

Chapter 13

His Cruel Mind

He didn't remember falling asleep at all, yet he woke up startled at the sound of Juan yelling his name. He was still holding the stick in his hands and his etches were spread out before him in the dirt. He didn't feel rested, it must have only been minutes. Arthur was already dressed, same clothes as yesterday, so he straightened them out while smoothing his hair. Funny thing about this man, in spite of all the secrets in his life if he was going to be around Juan, he better look decent.
Appearances meant everything to Juan for the life of illusions that they lived. He peeked out of his hole carefully, making sure Juan did not see him step out of his hiding place. As he rounded the corner, their eyes locked. The dark, sinister eyes staring back at him left Arthur breathless.

The silence was the worst part about the drive... quiet tears slid down Arthur's cheeks and he was once again that terrified little boy. Try as he might, he couldn't stop his body from shaking or his thoughts from spinning out of control. Arthur said, "I was sure this would be the day Juan killed me or left me far away because no one knew I left with him." Instead, Juan parked the truck in a busy, dirty part of town and they walked down an alley. Arthur had no idea where he was... The whole area reeked of liquor and smoke. Arthur frantically searched out the buildings, looking for a spot to hide or get help if he needed to. He didn't understand why Juan dragged him here. Why did he always look to hurt him? What else could he do to please this man? Arthur couldn't take it anymore and blurted out, "please let me go, I will work harder and eat less." Those words stopped Juan. He stared at Arthur for a few seconds, though it seemed like an eternity, and smirked. Arthur hadn't noticed that they had arrived at a house until he heard a gentle 'hello.' He stared blankly at this overly made up face. The look was familiar...tired, empty, lifeless eyes and a frozen smile.

Juan shoved Arthur into the front door, handing him a wad of money as he said, "I will be back cavron." Arthur was terrified, hardly breathing-his feet glued to their spot. The door shut and this woman took hold of Arthur's arm and gently moved him forward. She walked him to a dirty, dark, small cubicle and told him to undress. As his eyes adjusted to the dark, Arthur could see walls with stains all over them and a dingy mattress on the floor. Alongside the bed on the floor sat a pretty, colorful pitcher filled with water and lemons floating in it. He thought it odd, it looked out of place in this filthy room, much like he felt. Arthur knew this was like the place his father once owned. He tried to drown out the noises, but the noise in his head was unstoppable. This young boy slid down the wall and curled up into a ball, drawing his knees to his chest and hugged them tight. The sound of his own teeth chattering was deafening. He needed to escape.

Eyes closed, he blocked out his thoughts and started pleading to the one his momma used to talk about, God. They didn't talk heaven in their home.

Was he real? Does he exist? It made Arthur sad to realize she must have given up and quit believing in him. Momma Mary nor Grandma Concha mentioned God anymore. Or did they? Arthur was busy and hardly spent anytime around them now, there were so many baby girls. His mind is all scrambled and his heart won't stop slamming against his chest wall... Reminds him of a conversation he overheard his teacher having about him with the school counselor. Ms Ganet was so kind, and concerned after Arthur told her that his heart always felt like it would explode. The counselor had mentioned 'anxiety attacks' and how pills might help...lost in thought, the opening of the door startled him... He found himself staring into the same, sad face and she motioned to him to get up. She gently grabbed his arm and walked him out the same way he had come in and shut the door. Just like that he was standing outside all alone. Much to Arthur's relief, Juan was nowhere in sight. He started walking aimlessly, hoping it was in the right direction. Panic sets in as he starts feeling like he can't escape. His walking turns into running fast and furious. It's his own skin he is trying to escape...

The blaring horn jolted him and Arthur quit running. His eyes slowly shift sideways--afraid to look into Juan's mean, black eyes. Instead, a kind looking older gentleman asked if he was alright. "I'm trying to get home," Arthur said. He offered him a ride and Arthur didn't hesitate, he jumped into the truck. This young boy did not fear much, only his father. He was able to describe the area he lived in and once they got closer to it, Arthur asked to be let out. He knew better than to run the risk of Juan catching someone giving him a ride anywhere. He made it home and wanted to hug Grandma Concha.

Lights were on but it was very quiet. Either Juan was there and everyone scattered, not wanting to cross his path, or he'd already been there and left and they were still hiding. Quietly entering the barracks, Arthur looks around, he is very hungry. He had not eaten today. He took his chances and grabbed as many biscuits as he could hold. Grandma Concha grabbed him from behind and pulled him into one of the rooms. She told him to eat and motioned to be quiet, than put him in the closet and closed the door. Arthur knew Juan was here. He couldn't eat the warm biscuits now. He strained to hear what was going on. The older girls and Grandma Concha were trying to keep the younger ones quiet, but that was proving to be a difficult task. Than he heard it...a quiet muffled cry. Arthur knew Juan had his momma and those sounds devastated him. He would give anything to protect her. The absence of fear startles him. If the house wasn't filled with all his sisters and grandma, he knew in his heart he could hurt this man.
These kinds of episodes cause him to go deeper into the recesses of his mind, the only place he feels safe. He would shut down a part of himself that would never emerge again. Though it would hinder his ability to love freely and completely, it proved to be his saving grace. Not wanting to hear his momma whimper or beg this man to stop, Arthur

opened the closet door and walked out. He was half hoping Juan would be right there and Juan would have to face his wrath...secretly Arthur was relieved no one was in sight.

Chapter 14

Kindness Exists

Each new day brought no relief, much the same as the day before--beatings, hunger and dodging Juan. Work was always welcomed...losing himself in it-his imagination allowed his heavy heart to be free. One day rolled into the next and Arthur was always surprised when seasons changed. The cold had somehow disappeared and spring was upon them. The sound of nature caught his ear and he smiled. He knew it meant baby animals would be arriving and Arthur dashed off. In spite of life, he was still a child. There was a farm down the road with pigs, goats and cows. If he were lucky, he could milk the cows and have fresh milk. He salivated at the thought of it. As he rounded the corner, he saw the farmer outside with the animals. Arthur stood and watched from afar.

The man waved him over and asked if he wanted to help. He needed no coaxing or instruction, Arthur had milked many a cow, to stave off hunger. He went right to work and the farmer enjoyed watching him. After Arthur had milked several cows, played around with the goats and fed baby pigs, he sat down genuinely happy. That was a rare happening.

The farmer handed him a cup of fresh milk and Arthur gulped it down quickly. The farmer asked him where he was from and what he did for fun. Without hesitation, he told him, "I'm not from anywhere and I work for fun." He told Arthur he was welcome to help out and play with the animals for fun and drink all the milk he wanted. He smiled a big, heartfelt smile, knowing this farmer meant what he said. Arthur was surprised but loved the joy he felt inside.

The walk home was pleasant. Arthur was not hungry, satisfied from the milk and the idea of a new place to escape. The thought of it was a welcomed reprieve. Lately, his thoughts were scaring him. He was not afraid of Juan, as much as he was angry at him. Arthur was looking for a change. He needed more than this life in Arvin.

Days passed, spring was becoming summer and Arthur was enjoying his time at the farmers ranch after work. The kind man sent Arthur home with a full jug of fresh milk. He couldn't wait to share it...he walked in looking for Grandma Concha and held it up smiling. She was as excited as he was about the milk. Grandma didn't question where it came from, she simply enjoyed it. His happiness always warmed her heart. It was short lived. Grandma Concha(connie) told Arthur that momma Mary was having another baby. His eyes said it all and she hugged him, convincing them both that it would be alright. Her heart broke for her little girl, wondering when it would all end...12 children and no end in sight. Connie closed her eyes and inhaled deeply, tears rolling down her cheeks, Arthur gently wiped them away. He knew about the children she had been forced to leave behind and wondered if she was crying for them, for herself or for momma Mary. He hoped it wasn't for him, that thought made him stand straighter and tell her with such confidence, "things will be fine," he almost believed it himself.

As usual, time marched on by, and changes abound. The younger girls were working in the fields more often now and it caused extra stress for Arthur. He worried about the older ones that flirted with the men and the younger ones who were clueless about them. His momma was showing now, her belly ripe with the child growing inside. Work was becoming more difficult for her by the day. The cold weather always froze the fingers, making the job of picking cotton quite challenging. But they all knew they had better work hard and fast. Cold, heat, rain nor snow were ever an excuse for slowing down... His moods more unpredictable than usual. Juan always became angrier and meaner as his momma's belly grew. It happened each time and it puzzled Arthur...why so many children if you hate them? Why have two wives if you hate them? Arthur knew he'd treasure his own kids and wife one day. They'd never work nor be afraid of him...Arthur hoped he'd have lots of boys to love. His biggest dream was to have a son who would love him. The ringing of the bell pulled Arthur out of his daydreams. The work day was over and he made sure each sister turned in the bags and paper slips to get paid. He collected the monies for Juan and walked them all home, holding his momma by the arm. Her back hurt by the end of the day whenever she was with child...and that seemed to be always.

The wind was slapping against them and they huddled closer together, walking as fast as they could. Juan pulled up and everyone piled into the truck. It was silent as they all watched to see if Arthur would be allowed to join them. Juan reeked of liquor and bellowed "get in." Arthur jumped into the truck bed and smiled, so grateful for the ride.

As they pulled up to the barracks, Arthur saw some men sitting outside and dread overcame him. His first thought was about Grandma Concha...was she alright? Than he worried about the girls, were they here for them? Arthur ran into the house, unaware of what anyone else was doing. Connie looked up and smiled at him, the baby girls all around her. She was a mess, but safe. There was food for the girls on the counter, clothes laying over the chair to be mended and eggs in a basket that she had collected for the day. The barracks were spotless though. Even the dirt floors were clean. Everything had its' place or there would be hell to pay. Juan would not tolerate messes anywhere. That wasn't an easy task with 12 children in one home, even if the barracks were big.

Arthur walked over to Juan's spot and placed the money in the box-than left-very relieved everyone was alright. He knew better than to hang around with Juan there, especially intoxicated....he was hungry though. Grandma Concha looked out the window and watched him walking down the dirt road. She knew he was going off to his hidden spot, all alone, hungry and cold. It pained her...looking around for Juan, hoping he wasn't watching. She ran after her little guy and handed him a blanket. Hidden in the blanket was a roll and a small jar of milk. Arthur walked on feeling light hearted. He was grateful for a peaceful night and something to fill his tummy.

This young boy never took things for granted. He knew far to well how tumultuous life was. Stress was an everyday factor, a joy stealer. At this young age, he knew the importance of keeping his anxiety at bay. Tucking all his emotions away, he forged on, not giving in to the demons that shackled his life. He chose to believe that there was more to life than this. He was willing to fight for it.

Work was becoming more scarce. More and more men and their families were showing up to the fields looking for work. The foreman started parceling off sections of fields to different families, cutting their work in half. This did not make Juan very happy. Arthur knew something would change. His father did not sit around waiting for things to get better, he forced changes.

As time went on, Juan disappeared often, for long stretches. Arthur had no idea what he was up to, but he was curious. Things at home were not easy. Juan would come by and take the money, leaving nothing for food or necessities. Arthur never came home without finding something extra for the girls to eat. The farmer still allowed Arthur to take milk home, yet it was never enough. There were to many mouths to feed and to many bodies to dress. Momma Mary was big, Arthur thought she looked like a big ball ready to pop. It was miserably hot and he really worried about his momma working in it. He would soak rags with water and have her suck on them, hoping to keep her hydrated. Arthur had watched several men have heat strokes and it scared him. He was angry that the very man who had them in this situation was the same one that needed to help them...to many things going on for him to do it alone. Arthur wasn't making enough money to feed all his sisters, grandma, momma and keep Juan happy. So though he despised this man, he also desperately yearned for his approval and love...Juan did not care. He always took the money and ran, leaving Arthur to figure it out.

Grandma Concha(connie) was resourceful and would surprise Arthur with a piece of fresh bread. He knew she worried about him. At times he feels loved, but mostly he felt the burden she carried in her heart for him. The inner turmoil twisting and turning in his mind robbed Arthur of peace. The screaming was louder and louder in his head. Anger was harder to contain and Arthur was scratching to get out.

Chapter 15

Strength in Love

Arthur and Penny were thick as thieves. He felt comfortable sharing his fears, as well as his dreams with her. As his anger mounted, protecting her became his outlet. If any boys teased, flirted or looked at Penny the wrong way, Arthur would charge at them with all the strength an 11 year old, 80 pound kid could muster. He would start swinging at them, holding nothing back, releasing all his pent up emotions with a vengeance. It would shock the kids and they'd go running. Arthur was not afraid. Changes couldn't come soon enough.

Arthur was under the barracks feeding his animals, watering his garden and eating tomatoes when he heard the commotion. He climbed out of his special place and peeked out to see what was going on. Grandma Concha(Connie) was tearing sheets, his sister was running in with a bucket of water and he could hear momma Mary moaning. With a heavy sigh, he slid back into his private world. Laying down, he closed his eyes and knew what awaited him. Within hours, there would be another mouth to feed, another baby he'd love and have to protect. He cried himself to sleep, afraid there was no more of him to give.

A new day, a new attitude. Arthur jumped up, anxious to see if he had a baby brother. He looked around outside, Juan's truck was gone. He was relieved. The house was quiet, so he tiptoed in and almost tripped over his little sisters. Two of them were asleep on the kitchen floor. Grandma Concha(connie) was not around, which was unusual, especially since Mary had just had her baby. It was grandma who took over the babies and became like the mom...not this time. There sat momma Mary, holding this beautiful baby girl. She motioned him over and said "kiss your new sister--Geena." Arthur was surprised that he was once again mesmerized by this new life. He leaned over and gently kissed her forehead, touching her soft cheek, sad for what lie ahead of her. Mary could see the questions in his eyes and told him, "Juan took Connie with him and I don't know why. He is planning something. Don't worry mijo." All Arthur could do was worry. He loved his Grandma Concha(Connie) more than anything and couldn't imagine life without her. He pleaded to that elusive God high in the sky, "please save my grandma from him." Arthur went off to work with knots in his stomach and a hope that he'd see her again.

As it turns out, several days would go by without a word from Juan. Mary tried to act like she wasn't worried, but her bright blue eyes betrayed her. Arthur would walk through the town of Arvin, after work, hoping to catch a glimpse of Juan's truck. Everyone had the same thoughts going through their mind, but did not speak their fears out loud. Arthur walked into the house on the third or fourth day that grandma had disappeared with Juan. He looked around and kicked a chair angrily, startling momma Mary and his sisters. He walked back out the door slamming it shut. Mary held Geena tightly in her arms, snuggling her while she could. This was a rare treat for her. She was always back to work within two days of giving birth to her children. Mary strained forward to see where her troubled son was going. Her heart grieved as she watched him punch a tree over and over again, until his hands were red, covered in blood. Silent prayers filled her mind, asking God to bring her momma back. Mary understood exactly what Connie meant to her boy.

The new day brought answers to their prayers. On any other day, the sound of Juan's truck driving up caused fear. Today it caused panic of a new kind, hope that Grandma Concha(connie) would be sitting in that truck. Mary scurried to the window, breath held, she let out a cry when she saw her opening the truck door. Her little girls looked at her confused. No matter that her momma moved gingerly and had a black eye, she was alive. Mary realized how scary it would be facing this man everyday without her around.

Connie(concha) walked in and smiled. She always wore that smile, aware of her role in keeping the calm in their storm. She announced to Mary and anyone listening, "Juan has found a new place we will be moving to Bakersfield. Start packing up, we leave immediately." No one asked questions, they did as they were told, packing up quickly and efficiently. The younger girls and Grandma Concha put everything in the back of the truck while Juan watched drinking his beer.

Arthur and his older sisters could see the top of the truck from afar. He took off running and kept stumbling. In his haste to catch a glimpse of his grandma, his feet were outrunning his body. As soon as he saw the girls loading up the truck, he couldn't catch his breath. He thought they were going to be on the run again because Juan had done something horrible to his precious grandma. But there she stood, smiling at him, with a knowing look that only Arthur understood. Tears covered his cheeks at the sight of her. Though there would be no hug or words exchanged, their silent look and smile at one another said a thousand words...

Much like their lives, these two woman with 12 children, disappeared into the night without anyone noticing. Arthur's heart was heavy and excited. He was worried about what would become of his animals and sad to leave his private oasis, yet open and ready for changes. He was following behind Juan's truck in some man's large vehicle, surrounded by goats. Arthur loved animals and felt at home. He believed he loved them more than momma Mary and his sisters. Grandma Concha(Connie) held a special place in his heart. He was not afraid to love her.

Jostled awake by loud voices, Arthur was scared and confused. He'd forgotten they had moved. He gently moved the goats and jumped out of the truck. Juan was arguing with the driver of the truck. Grandma Concha called Arthur over and he joined his sisters sitting on the curb. All their meager belongings were stacked up neatly on the ground. Arthur was getting the distinct feeling that things didn't turn out as Juan planned, now they had no where to go...he daydreamed about the only other time he'd been to Bakersfield before. It was the marble competition and he was attending school. How long ago was that? It seemed like a very long time ago when he was very young. Not for the first time, Arthur wondered how old he actually was... crying babies brought Arthur back to the present.

Chapter 16

New Horizons...still the same

It was late, the young girls wanted to be held so they could sleep, and Gracie was crying because she was hungry. Momma Mary tried quieting her newborn by feeding her. Grandma Concha led the girls to a small, open field. The older sisters helped her settle the young ones and Arthur carried over all their belongings. He was unsettled and worried what the new day would bring. All he wanted now was Arvin. Grandma spread out blankets, laid the girls down and covered them with towels. Arthur took one spot at the end, his momma at the other side and he tried to sleep. This reminded him of days gone by. The only difference now, they had tripled in numbers, girls everywhere. Of course, Juan had taken off and left them there...

Needless to say, it was a sleepless night for Arthur. He had dreamed of returning to the town where he'd had the best experience of his life--the steely marble competition. This was not what he expected, though he accepted whatever came his way with a good attitude. He was walking the town looking for food for his family.

At the corner stood an old brick building with an enticing aroma which caught Arthur's attention. An older woman was holding a bag and walking toward the trash bins. Arthur was also walking toward the bins when they caught each others eye. Again, that comforting feeling came over him. All at once, Arthur knew things would be alright. He would find food and a place for his family. This woman handed him the bag she was holding, smiled, and walked back to the bakery. He opened the bag and jumped up with excitement. Arthur raced back to his flock of girls as proud as he could be.

Grandma Concha(Connie) already had everyone dressed and had set up a temporary camp. She amazed Arthur and he felt hopeful when he watched her. He handed out rolls, muffins and bagels to his very excited sisters. Grandma patted his back and he could feel her gratefulness. Arthur asked her, "what are the plans? Should I start looking for a place to stay now?" She shook her head no, telling him work was more important. He agreed.

Arthur had no idea where to look for work, this town was much bigger than he was used to. He decided to walk around and familiarize himself with it. Something about Bakersfield made him smile. He didn't know why but it felt good. Maybe it was the friendliness of strangers...or the fact that it appeared most families lived in real homes...there were houses everywhere...whatever it was, he was ready for it. With hope and a lightness to him that he'd never felt, he set off to find work. Arthur approached strangers offering to clean windows, cars, pick up trash-anything that came to mind. This worked for the moment, and Arthur was grateful to be able to help Grandma Concha(Connie) buy food. Juan, strangely enough, did not seem to be in much of a hurry to put him to work.

Juan came and went quickly, staying long enough to harass his grandma, momma and him. Nothing was good enough for this man. Ever. It never even occurred to Juan to ask how they were surviving and eating... He knew full well that he had dumped them in a strange town with no housing or work. This infuriated Arthur. Luckily, he had inherited his father's tenacity. He was a survivor. Juan was angry when he would show up and there was no meat or liquor. In order to protect his momma's from Juan's wrath, Arthur started stealing the things he knew Juan would expect to find whenever he arrived. Though he felt bad taking from people who showed him kindness, there was no other way to appease this man. The girls weren't working yet, and Arthur could barely put food on the table to feed the family. Most days, Arthur lived off scraps and went hungry.

Grandma Concha had found an old abandoned shed that they turned into a home. There was a lot of grumbling by the older girls. They were not happy with this new situation they found themselves in. Arthur wondered why they bothered complaining, but as they got older, he noticed it was happening often. One afternoon, his older sister Ana was griping out loud, to no one in particular, but Juan happened to walk in on her tirade. He confronted her about it, and much to everyone's surprise, Ana stood up to him. She said, "I hate living here. Why are we here with no where to stay?" Juan picked up a broom and slammed it across her face, breaking her nose... Grandma Concha(Connie) ran to Ana cleaning her up. Arthur got weak in the knees. This was the first time he was that violent with the girls. It would not be the last. Ana would change after this incident, angry and tired of this man. She would challenge him on many occasions. Arthur worried, rightfully, that if he couldn't stop his sister from speaking her mind to Juan, he would pay a mighty price.

Luckily, after a few weeks, Juan found steady work for them. Arthur liked working. It kept him away from home and relaxed him. He had trouble sitting still. Cotton picking was the only joy in his life. Arthur recognized the area, knowing it must be close to the Edison rancher they had stayed with at one time. Those were good memories. He knew the rancher had wanted to protect them and send them far away before Juan had arrived from Mexico. This man had fallen in love with his momma. Arthur had overheard the conversation between his momma and the rancher. But his momma was terrified that Juan would kill Grandma Concha and the other kids if they disappeared. So here they were, still running place to place and surviving the wrath of Juan.

Arthur was scared and felt very alone, he knew he needed to go find a new place to escape to. He missed his old hideaway with the animals, garden and peace of mind he had discovered. So began another journey of Arthur's life. Tears slipped down his face as he walked toward the cotton fields. He knew he needed an attitude change or the day would be impossible to get through.

As time went on, Arthur became known for his uncanny ability to pick cotton so quickly and efficiently. He outworked everyone, grown men and women. Though he was growing, now around age 12 he believed, Arthur was very thin and wiry. The bags of cotton far outweighed his child like frame. Arthur never gave that a thought, he set his mind to do whatever was put in front of him. Plus, he loved the attention his cotton picking skills gave him.

Life for the Rodriguez family was more chaotic than usual. They were still stuck in this over sized shed- to many bodies in one spot. The weather was changing and Arthur wondered how they'd ever stay warm in this place with no windows or sealed doors. There were so many little ones to be concerned about, it frightened Arthur. The walk to the fields was also very long and becoming quite difficult. Ana started voicing her thoughts about this often, and it would put the whole family on edge. Even the younger girls understood their sisters' complaints would unleash a rage in Juan. They had witnessed enough of it already...Arthur would gather the young ones together-hoping it would help them feel safe. He just couldn't figure out why Ana provoked Juan on purpose. It was only a matter of time before she would suffer the consequences, once again, for speaking without permission.

Everyone was hungry, tired, moody and cold. Grandma Concha(connie) and momma Mary had been overly edgy because Juan kept coming back and taking Penny with him. Without a word from Juan, he'd return her. Arthur would always ask her if she was alright, Penny always said yes. It angered Ana and she'd had enough. Arthur begged her to leave things be but she went to Juan anyway. Before she could finish her first sentence, Juan slapped her with such force she fell back. The look on her face was one of shock, blood oozing from her mouth and tears rolling down her face. Arthur wondered why she was surprised. Of course, he realized they were not so accustomed to beatings, as he was. The little ones started crying and scattered everywhere, so grandma and momma gathered them up...reminding Arthur of his old momma hens gathering their baby chicks when they were frightened back in Arvin.

Juan punched, kicked and dragged Ana through the shed. Arthur tried to distract Juan, screaming at him to stop. He jumped on Juan's back hoping his sister would run. He threw Arthur across the room and laughed, leaving Angel curled up in a ball on the floor. Arthur sat on the floor, heaving deep breaths, feeling anger seep into every bone of his body. He crawled over to check on his sister but she wanted nothing to do with him or anyone else. Even Grandma Concha and momma Mary left her alone. Arthur was so mad at Ana for not listening. He hated all of them...After a few days, just like the physical markings disappeared from Ana.s face, legs and arms--so did the incident from everyone's mind. Life went on as usual.

Grandma Concha(Connie) and Arthur were outside the shed building a fire. They were trying to find ways to keep the girls warm when they heard yelling. It was Juan and a Filipino man arguing. Juan hit him with a wooden board when the man told him he wanted Penny now, instead of in a year. Though this man was much larger than Juan, he kept on fighting. The fact that his father feared no one terrified Arthur. Grandma Concha grabbed Arthur and ran into the shed, as Juan hit the man again. Everyone stood silent-waiting to see what would happen next. Momma Mary was crying and holding Penny. Arthur wasn't certain, but figured out that his father must have given Penny to this man. That would explain why he kept taking her.

Juan walked into the shed, threw a small black bag at Grandma Concha and walked out. No one breathed a word. Once they knew Juan was gone, momma Mary walked over to Connie and hugged her. It was a rare sight, they never touched... But they knew how lucky they were to have Penny there. Unbeknownst to the rest of the family, Juan had sold his daughter to this man for 3500 dollars to be his wife. Something went wrong with their agreement and Juan ended up with both money and daughter. Arthur wasn't surprised, Juan always got his way. He was so grateful his sister wouldn't be leaving. Fear had a strong grip on his mind. He never thought Juan would get rid of the girls, just him... This realization haunted him.

As usual, this incident was quietly stored away in the recesses of Arthur's mind, never to be thought of or spoken of again. But each of these events would shape his life forever. The constant battle of good versus evil and hope versus despair would rage in his mind, always trying to take over his thoughts. Arthur would continue to fight hard at the tender age of 12, always rising above it.

He wasn't sure what he thought of Bakersfield yet. Life here had been much more difficult than he hoped. Arthur loved the farmland though. It stretched out as far as his eyes could see. The massive land of green against the brown mountains made a beautiful sight. He would get lost in the beauty of it. Nature was his escape. Arthur was lucky enough to have met some men in the fields who offered to give him rides to and from work. That made his mornings so much easier because he really was on his own now. Feeling the disappointment and sting as well, Grandma Concha had so many girls to contend with, she was no longer able to give Arthur much time or attention. He had to try and find his own scraps of food since she no longer gathered things for him. Yes, he knew the ride was a blessing and appreciated it. She still made sure to give him her sweet smile and a hug whenever she could.

One day after work, Arthur was finding his way back to the shed slowly. They could only give him a ride near the area of the shed. Exploring was always something Arthur enjoyed. The human spirit, sometimes more resilient than one realizes, that little boy still existed within him. Relishing this rare occasion, moments turned into hours...losing track of time. It was dark before he knew it. Looking around, a momentary panic attack took over because nothing looked familiar. But there it stood, on the left hand corner, a big flashing, orange neon sign hanging on this abandoned building that was falling apart. He had no idea what it said, but the flashing sign kept him awake at night. Arthur wanted to go in and explore it badly. There was something about the building that scared him. The dilapidated structure, such a forlorn figure, struck a chord within him. He ran home never looking back.

As he walked into the shed and looked around- a sense of dread filled him from head to toe... The silence was deafening. In its' empty state the shed looked eerie. His thoughts spinning out of control he wondered where everyone was. Had they finally abandoned him? He sat down on the floor quietly, pools of water filling his eyes. Arthur closed them, shutting everything out, tears soaking his face. He allowed his mind to take him to happier places...Arthur could feel the moist dirt, smell the sweet aroma of corn still hanging on the stalks and hear the natural sounds of nature. Birds chirping, frogs croaking, ducks quacking...he could even see the beautifully colored green and orange caterpillars that he was fascinated by, crawling down the cornstalk. He wished to stay right there in his mind...Safe, unafraid and not alone.

The crunching of the gravel caught his ear. Every muscle in his body tensed up. He wanted to crawl into the walls but there was no where to go, no where to hide in this empty shed. Eyes sealed shut, Arthur flinched at the touch on his arm until he recognized Grandma Concha's weathered, dry but gentle hand. He put his hand over hers and smiled. She was kneeling bedside him, staring intently, but smiling a sweet, though sad smile. Wiping his cheeks dry with her hands, she stood up and pulled Arthur to his feet. Arm around his shoulder Grandma Concha said, "oh my mijo." Arthur was so relieved she came to get him. He couldn't help but wonder, if not for her, would Juan have abandoned him here...he was certain he knew the unspoken truths.

The walk seemed fairly quick. It was actually several miles away and they'd been walking for some time. Arthur wanted to ask his grandma if Juan sent for him or if she had to sneak over? Instead, he soaked up their surroundings, breathing in deeply, feeling giddy with excitement. He didn't know why. As horrible as life with Juan was Arthur needed to belong somewhere. Feeling light, free and as if he had just narrowly escaped his biggest fear, Arthur skipped ahead of Grandma Concha.

To any passerby, these two appeared as normal as could be. A sweet grandma on a walk with her happy, carefree grandson...if anyone knew the horrors these two faced every day they would find it hard to accept, much less believe.

Chapter 17

A House but not a Home

There it stood, a real house with a big yard and green grass all around. Fruit trees spread out that he recognized immediately, crab apple, orange trees-as well as a few pecan trees and grape vines. The house looked to small for the property it sat on. The dark brown trim and off white paint made it look warm and inviting though. Arthur saw several bunnies scurrying on his right side through the yard. A lump caught in his throat, a well of tears ready to break loose. So many questions... What did this mean? He had seen many homes that looked like this with children running around--playing, laughing and parents sitting around watching them. Could this happen to him? Would he get to enjoy the yard, play and hang out with his grandma?

It didn't take but a moment for Arthur to realize life would remain the same. As he and Grandma Concha walked into the new house, Juan slapped his sweet, unsuspecting grandma across the face. He yelled at her, "where did you go? The girls need you here." The chatter between the girls was silenced and the usual tension permeated the walls of their new home. With that, Juan grabbed momma Mary, pushed her into a room and shut the door. Arthur assumed it must be a bedroom and his was heart heavy. He knew if nothing changes, than nothing changes.

Grandma Concha walked toward Arthur, but he put his hand up to stop her. He could never be rude to her but he was in no mood to be nice or sympathetic. Arthur needed to walk, he was angry, really angry at everyone. He left, shutting the door quietly while his mind was screaming loudly. He noticed he was angrier more often now. Grandma told him that was normal at age 12 and a half....well that explanation only frustrated him more. Didn't anyone in his family see what he saw? Nothing was normal. He wasn't even sure what normal was supposed to look like anymore. Any illusions, dreams or hopes he secretly daydreamed about his family had died.

He liked the backyard. It was big enough to have his own garden and animals, if he could hide it from Juan. The sun was setting and the tall pecan trees had his full attention. Arthur climbed it effortlessly and felt at ease immediately. He liked his new spot a lot.

Momma Mary was calling Arthur's name. He wanted to stay right there, ignore her, and climb up higher. Of course there would be no ignoring his momma or climbing any higher. Instead, he jumped down startling her. Into the house they went. He smiled at the usual chaos. Arthur didn't realize that a loud, noisy house was comforting to him. It meant Juan was not around. His mommas had done a nice job setting up the house.

Arthur was excited to look around. There was a real kitchen with a stove like he had seen before in food places, a toilet, which meant no more digging holes and two bedrooms. He thought it was funny that both rooms connected to the bathroom. Arthur was surprised with the big room next to the kitchen, wondering what the purpose of it was for. He liked the house.

Settling down for the night would have been challenging for most families, but these 11 kids and Grandma Concha crunched into one of the small bedrooms. They were spread all over the floor, side by side, used to these sleeping arrangements. Legs and arms intertwined...not able to tell one from the other. There was no such thing as personal space for this family. Momma Mary and her youngest child, Geena, were in the other room. Arthur was sickened for her, stuck in a room where the crazy, vicious man would show up.

A regular routine became commonplace for the Rodriguez family in this new home, though there was nothing normal in their daily lives. In the midst of everyday people, living all around them, Arthur and his family endured horrible abuse silently. Juan had such power and control over these two woman and kids that no one dared to speak out against him...

Juan did make a point of telling Arthur and the older girls to get to work. He even taught them the route to take. They were quite a distance from the cotton fields. Strangely enough, he no longer showed up there to check on them or help out at all. He would disappear for days, show up to sleep for a day than harass and terrorize them before vanishing. But not before telling Arthur that he did not want to see him around the house anymore, other than to turn over the wages earned. Juan said in his half English-half Spanish way of speaking, "cavron, you are a disgrace, you shame me... sustantivo(embarrassment)--stay out of my sight." His words were cruel and cut like a sharp knife, deep into his soul.

Arthur refused to cry. He hated this man but he wanted to feel nothing. He walked outside and without thinking, Arthur started pounding the pecan tree, his fists were flailing wildly. He would pick up dirt and throw it, his tears turning his cheeks brown as he wiped them with muddy hands. Exhausted he kicked the tree and screamed. The strong grip of Juan flipped Arthur around. "Come on cavron, you wish that tree was me...hit me, hit me!" The more he taunted Arthur, the more he shut down. Fear gripped him like a vise clamping down. Juan was calm with that eerie smile he was known to give them. It was the look Arthur had nightmares about. He watched Juan walk away and return with that very thick rope. The last thing he remembers is Juan telling him not to move.

He beat Arthur until he was weak with pain and curled up on the ground. Eyes closed, he waited for the next blow...instead it was still and quiet, except for Juan's labored breathing. One thing Arthur noticed lately, Juan's strength did not last as long. He grew weary much quicker, the beatings took a lot out of him. Or was he getting soft...possibly feeling bad about his treatment toward him? Whatever it was, Arthur hoped it was over. Both mommas were peering out the kitchen window. As soon as he threw the rope down and walked away, Connie(grandma) went running to Arthur. She gently jostled him until he opened his eyes. They walked into the kitchen where she gave him some freshly churned butter milk to drink and cleaned him up. As he watched her hide the rope deep into the pantry, his body involuntarily shook, knowing far to well how much pain it could inflict on him. Arthur wanted to lay down and just sleep. His body hurt all over--welts popping up on his legs, arms and chest.

Grandma Concha(Connie) walked Arthur outside to the backyard, all the way to the left side of the yard. He had noticed this small garage type of building but had not gone in there. She didn't say much, just nodded in the direction of the garage. Arthur walked in and looked around. In one corner stood a little cot and a bucket. He had no idea if this was supposed to be a punishment but he welcomed it. He would be away from Juan. The sight of the bucket was even a happy sight...better than digging a hole during the night. All Grandma Concha said was, "this is best for now." She didn't have to worry, Arthur could not agree more.

Left alone with his thoughts Arthur looked around and decided he would make a home for animals again. He was so grateful for his grandma...there in the corner, neatly folded, sat an extra blanket and a biscuit. He realized he was hungry and ate it quickly, than laid down. He knew the weather was changing because he could not get warm. Feeling lost, scared and angry he cried himself to sleep...not seeing an end in sight to this life.

Waking up to the sound of roosters crowing was very comforting. Arthur jumped up, got dressed and took off on foot to work. He remembered the route. It was strange to not see any family before leaving but he did not want to run the risk of seeing Juan. He wondered what this man did all day now that he never showed up to work. Something was different about Juan. His looks were changing. His eyes were always red. They looked like pools of blood to Arthur, reminding him of his old pet pig. Arthur had loved this animal. He was so surprised Juan allowed him to have this pet that he never named it. He did not trust Juan and thought leaving the pig nameless would prevent him from becoming to attached to it. Arthur found out he was wrong.

One day while he was chasing his pig around and laughing, Juan walked over to Arthur, handed him a shot gun and told him to shoot it. He was so shocked at the order, Arthur said no while shaking his head emphatically. Angered, Juan grabbed his pig and held it tightly by the neck. He shoved it in Arthur's face and told him to watch...his pig was squealing and as if the pig knew what Juan had planned--its' eyes were bulging out and blood red. Boom. The shot rang out echoing in Arthur's ears. Moments passed in silence. Than Juan told him to clean up. Arthur had not realized blood had splattered all over him... Arthur kept on walking to work and tried to clear his mind of the image that lingered. Yes, Juan's looks were changing. His hair was turning more and more white. Arthur couldn't wait to get to work so he could quit thinking. He ran as fast as his feet could move.

The distance from his home was far to much to get there on time. He started asking strangers for rides. Luck was on his side and a kind man agreed to take him to the cotton fields. Arthur never knew how to react to another man, especially when they were nice. Though this gentleman attempted to make small talk--asking him his age, where his family was, did he go to school...Arthur remained tight lipped, always fearful to divulge any personal information. As he was coming to a stop to let Arthur out, he offered to give him a ride any morning he needed it. Arthur knew this man felt bad for him, possibly worried about him...just like the Edison rancher and his teacher used to be. But he saw no point in allowing anyone to really help him out. Juan would put a stop to it. No one could stop Juan. He did whatever he wanted--why bother?

As days passed, Arthur fended for himself, finding ways to eat, get to work and stay warm. One particular Saturday, Juan wanted Arthur to go find wood to warm up the house. He had no idea where to start looking. He took off on foot and walked a few blocks. He decided he would have to steal the wood if he found any. It always bothered him to steal but he knew no other way to please his father. What this man wanted he got. Juan never gave Arthur any money when he sent him to do things that required it. After several more blocks, a panic started to well up within him. He wasn't having any success in finding wood. He popped into a soda shop to ask for help. Immediately the aroma of baked goods and ice cream caught his senses. His mouth watered and he was aware of his stomach growling with hunger. Arthur had learned to ignore such things, but in the midst of this heavenly place his body was at full attention, his senses betraying him. He quickly forgot about the task at hand.

Arthur stood out in this family environment. He was poorly dressed, very thin and barefoot, but mainly, he was alone. His big, droopy, kind, greenish brown eyes were hard to miss. He never said a word, Arthur just kept staring at all the baked goods and breathing it in deeply. He had never seen such an assortment of goodies all in one spot. His eyes slowly took in the scenery of the parents enjoying ice cream and laughing with their children. It mesmerized him. He never even heard the waitress asking if she could help him, not until she was upon him and handing him an ice cream cone. All at once he remembered why he walked into this soda shop... Arthur grabbed his cone and in between ravenous bites he asked, "how do I find wood for fire?" She explained as best she could, but was aware he was confused. So she pointed to the bus pulling up, handed him two coins and told him the bus driver could get him there.

Chapter 18

The Madness Continues

Arthur got onto the bus sitting right up front by the driver. He wiped the ice cream off his face with his sleeve and sat back hoping the man knew where to take him. After a couple of hours, Arthur was done sight seeing. He was antsy and could sense the driver watching him from the big mirror hanging in front of him. It was getting dark and the bus was almost empty. He had watched the people, one by one, exit the bus, climb down the steps and bid the driver a good night. The driver appeared to like that smiling at each person and chuckling. Finally, it is just Arthur, nothing looks familiar. He is looking down at his lap, hands bound tightly together and crying quietly. He doesn't know what to do. The bus comes to a slow stop and the driver asks, "how can I help you son?" The fact that he called him son so nicely really bothered Arthur. He was used to his life. The kindness from strangers was hard to accept or understand. Through tears Arthur explained where he lived as best he could. For the next couple of hours this man took the time to drive all over Bakersfield until they found Arthur's home. He thanked him several times, than stood frozen on the steps of the bus, afraid to face the consequences at home. Arthur had been gone about eight hours, lost for six and he had no wood to show for it. He knew this wouldn't end well for him.

Much to his surprise, Arthur heard laughter and lots of commotion going on. As he focused on the people through the living room window he forgot about the kind bus driver and took off running. He even forgot about his fears in his excitement to get inside. There stood his married sister Donna, Jake and his half-siblings, Joey and Vivian. Arthur was so happy to see Donna and gave her a big bear hug. So many questions came to mind but he asked none, shocked she was actually here. He assumed that he would never see her again. All the chatter and excitement continued. Arthur looked around catching momma Mary's empty smile in contrast to Grandma Concha's beaming face. Though her face was permanently etched with every pain she had endured in this life, her smile was real. Arthur appreciated her more than she would ever know.

Vivian and Joey were standing off by themselves, until Arthur arrived. These three had a special bond, an understanding of sorts. They knew the emptiness of belonging no where, unwanted and unloved. Juan stared them down without a word. After he walked out Arthur gave them a quick hug sensing how uncomfortable they were. Donna announced she was pregnant and was very excited. Arthur envied her. He wanted something of his own too. Grandma Concha cleared her throat to get everyone's attention-than said the three words Arthur had grown to hate- Mary is pregnant. It disgusted him. She was enslaved to this man and he made sure she was always with child. There was no cheering or congratulations, just an awkward silence. Arthur glanced at his momma who was looking down at her feet. Her look said all she never voiced. Shame. He wished he could tell her it would be alright as he walked out the house.

Arthur saw Joey and Vivian more often now. They did not return to Porterville with Donna and Jake. He wondered where they stayed but never asked. Time seemed to move at a faster pace in Bakersfield. His momma's ever growing tummy expanded overnight. She always looked cold in the fields-but she worked tirelessly in silence. Winters were harsh here and it affected his hands, slowing him down, which was not a good thing. Ever since Joey and Vivian returned Juan was everywhere. He worried that Juan would notice his hands giving him trouble. Almost every single morning he waited for Arthur to come out of the garage and greeted him with a balled up hand, tapping the top of his head as hard and fast as could with his knuckles. Juan would repeat this over and over, "you better work faster stupido(stupid)... apurate(hurry up)!" Tears stinging his cheeks as the cold hit against his soft boyish face, Arthur would quietly say ok. He would take off running, mentally exhausted, trying to find the strength to get through another day of Juan.

Some days Arthur had rides, other days he ran or would sneak onto a bus. He knew he needed to find a way to get to work regularly. Walking home from work one day, tule fog was setting in. He loved the feel and look of it. This was new to him and it was magical. In the middle of a yard, all alone, sat a shiny red bike. Without a second thought he ran to it, jumped on and pedaled away. He was angry at himself for taking it, angry for having nothing and feeling guilty. But he was so tired of trying to find ways to get around that by the time he arrived at home his guilt was gone. It was exhilarating to fly down the road with the wind whipping against his face, he felt free. Arthur hid the bike inside the garage far from Juan's prying eyes. His heart was beating wildly, he felt like it might jump out of his chest. Arthur didn't go in to see any family or look for food. He jumped into bed to calm himself. He was happy and terrified. Joy and misery come in pairs sometimes.

As soon as it was quiet, he got up and looked around. The house was dark, he peeked his face out the garage, straining to hear any voices. Silence. He rummaged through the garage and trash looking for something to scrape off the red paint. The thought made him sad but he knew the bike could not be recognized by anyone, or he would be in big trouble. It wasn't the law he worried about, it was Juan. Disguising the bike was crucial. Arthur stayed up all night until every drop of shiny red paint was gone. Only than would his story of finding it at a trash site be believable. Exhausted but happy, he put on three long sleeved t-shirts and rode off in the cold for work. He left extra early looking for a new route. Arthur was afraid to ride past the yard or see the kid who once owned this bike. He kept reminding himself that he deserved this bike...gnawing thoughts told him otherwise.

It wasn't as exhilarating as the first day riding it home. As each day passed, he wished he could take the bike back and leave it on that lawn. If it was still shiny red like the big fire trucks that intrigued him, no problem, but this bike looked nothing like that now. Arthur promised himself that he would never steal something like this again... Only necessities.

He could hear that familiar sound from quite a distance...high pitched, catlike cries. He could even imagine the little face turning redder with each wail. Arthur knew momma Mary must have had the baby. He jumped off the moving bike letting it fall to the ground. He knew this one might be the brother he was waiting for...eyes wide open, expectations high, Arthur never slowed down and stumbled into the room. As always, the softness in his momma's face and her bright blue eyes smiling gently as she gazed at her baby made him catch his breath. It was as it should be. Arthur knew his momma wanted to love him like that but couldn't. He closed his eyes, searing that image in his mind forever. Seeing that soft warm side of her gave him hope. There is nothing stronger than the power of hope. Momma Mary looked up, put her hand out and told Arthur to come meet his baby sister Nadra. At that moment, it didn't matter that it was another girl, 12 sisters, his momma smiled at him so sweetly he felt a lump in his throat. His body betraying him, his eyes moistening at her gentle touch on his hand, Arthur kissed Nadra quickly and left abruptly. He wanted to be loved so badly, it hurt physically and the weight of it all was crushing.

Another sister, another day...Arthur knew he needed to let it all go and focus on getting through the day. If there was any certainty in his life, he knew it was that life was hard. Things were constantly changing as he aged. One of the strangest things that changed was Juan's reaction to Arthur working. He still fist pounded his head every morning, yelling obscenities about going to work like a man, but it stopped there. His real obsession was now making sure that Arthur knew where each of his older sisters were and with whom at all times. Juan expected this done no matter what. Arthur felt much like a robot-set on auto mode. He would make sure each girl was home before leaving to work and that they were up and getting ready. They got to work later and usually had a ride. They also left work before Arthur so he would pedal home quickly to make sure they were all there. Juan told each one of them that he would beat Arthur and punish them if he did not know where they were at all times.

No one was happy about this arrangement, especially Ana. She made a point of sneaking away any time Arthur was busy. He was not surprised. He had noticed a guy walking away every time he was looking for Ana. As long as they both made it back to the house for Juan's eyes, Arthur did not care. He started getting careless about her. He would follow her on his bike but sneak back and hide in the garage. They all knew Juan would not be around. His new thing was gambling at this bar and drinking to excess. If they timed their comings and goings just right, he was none the wiser. By the time he came stumbling home and yelling for Connie and Mary to help him into the house, everyone was exactly where they were supposed to be. It is never wise to get that comfortable...

One morning after Arthur had made the rounds of checking on each sister, he went behind the garage. He was in the middle of building a large wooden cage for the bunnies he was going to collect. He heard the crunching of footsteps on the gravel. Frustrated, Arthur stepped out to the side to see who was going where. He had very few days off and was not happy that one of his sisters was interrupting it. Of course, it was Ana trying to step as gingerly as possible so she wouldn't be noticed. Hesitating, he almost jumped on his bike, but shrugged it off and went back to building his cage. He made a point of keeping an ear out for her return so he could walk her in. What neither Ana nor Arthur knew was that Juan had never left the house that day. Certain days he couldn't get out of bed after the previous night of partying. He was in a foul mood and watched Ana leave all on her own. Juan went looking for his rope, than sat down outside and waited.

If Arthur had not heard the laughing of Ana and Frank, he realized she had slipped his mind. Most of the day had somehow disappeared and the cage was done. He was proud of himself and excited to gather some new animals. First things first, he ran to meet Ana. He froze mid run, Juan looming large as life, the weight of his cruel hand holding Ana in place. The look on her face said what her silence couldn't. The rope dangling from his left hand caused him to tremble. Panic welled up in Arthur until he exploded.

He took off running and charged at Juan, unable to contain the hate, anger and fear toward this man. He beat Arthur with that rope until he was bloody. The sound of his sister yelling was silenced by a blow to the side of her head. Juan had thrown Arthur to the ground and now he was face to face with Ana. She was eerily still, lifeless-and he cried. The rope had ripped gashes into his legs, arms and torso. But the thought of his sister laying there was his only concern.

Juan walked away and came back with a bucket of water. Pouring it over Ana's face brought her back to the nightmare she had faded from. Bloody mouth, swollen cheek and lips--Ana was a sad mess to look at. Juan demanded to know why she snuck away without Arthur. She looked at Arthur, her eyes screaming for help...alone and scared. Her silence felt like an eternity. Ana finally spoke up. She explained that she was looking for a hall. There was going to be a dance that night and she wanted to attend it. Juan made her get up and told Arthur he would take her to the dance. Making an error in judgment , Ana said she no longer wanted to go. He slapped her hard causing Angel to scream, jumping up and down, until she fell to the ground sobbing. This young woman had taken more than she could handle. The human spirit has a breaking point. Juan walked away. Arthur knelt beside her gently rubbing her shoulder, trying to console her. He knew she would be going to this dance--bruised, busted mouth and all.

She believed she would die from a broken heart every time she had to clean Arthur up from his beatings. The hurt ran deeper than she ever imagined it could. What monster could inflict such cruelty to another human being...Grandma Concha(Connie) would never understand. She helped Ana look presentable, disguising the bruises as much as possible. Ana was humiliated that she was being forced to go now. But there he sat gloating. Arthur stole glances at Juan and wondered how this could make him feel good. Momma Mary stepped out of the room looking like a young girl herself--holding Nadra in one arm with Geena hanging onto her leg. Her expression revealed nothing. Arthur watched her stare blankly at Ana checking out her bruises. Those blue eyes betraying her stone face. Blinking quickly, tears forming, Mary hung her head. Without a word, the three of them disappeared back into the bedroom. Arthur felt defeated. They were the family with no voice. Silenced by the wrath of Juan.

The walk to the hall was long and arduous. Arthur felt the need to say something. He carried such guilt for allowing Juan to hurt his family. It wasn't like he forgot what Juan had said would happen, yet like so much of his life, Arthur had blocked it from his thoughts. He dared to play with fire. How could he stop it? Arthur imagined hurting him and ending his life in many different ways but he knew it would never be. Juan was unstoppable. The bond between these siblings ran deep. Ana could sense what Arthur was feeling. She draped her arm across his shoulders letting him know it was alright.

The night was cool, quiet, and clear. Arthur loved looking up at the sky twinkling with stars everywhere. Looking at all this gave him hope. It was back. That familiar feeling of someone watching over him would warm his body from head to toe. The peaceful evening ended as they approached the dance hall. Music was bumping and loud. Arthur could feel the vibration on the street. Young adults were everywhere...Smiling, laughter and enjoying themselves. It was not a common sight in his world. While he was looking around intrigued, Ana disappeared into the crowd of happy people.

He stood there alone and cold, unsure what to do with himself. But he knew he wouldn't leave and run the risk of not watching over Ana again. So he sat back and watched the comings and goings of these festive, young adults. It fascinated him to see people that had the freedom to laugh, talk and move around freely. As the night wore on, more and more men would step outside to smoke. They were loud and appeared drunk. Somehow they didn't frighten Arthur like Juan did. These men were having a good time. Arthur wondered if he would ever have the freedom to enjoy himself?

Sometime late in the evening Ana and Frank appeared in the doorway. She was smiling, yet there were tears in her eyes. Arthur jumped to his feet anger mounting within him, ready to defend and protect his sister. Instead Ana looked at him, her eyes dancing brightly and said nonchalantly, "I am getting married." Than they were off, those two walking through the streets without a care in the world. Smiling, touching, whispered conversations...Arthur envied the scene before him. He also panicked. Would they all get married, go away and leave him alone with Juan? It was not an image that settled well. He obviously had been lost in his thoughts, they were now in front of their

home. Frank gently touched Ana's face, kissing away each bruised spot. Arthur wondered if that was what love looked like--so elusive to him.

He couldn't seem to warm up, no matter how many layers of shirts he wore. The fog was thick and made his bike ride to work slow. Arthur was anxious to get there and start moving. He also knew if he got there early enough he might be one of the lucky ones to grab the free hot chocolate drinks the rancher passed out. His stomach was grumbling and it sounded so good. Arthur pedaled faster and faster. Though it was cold, he did enjoy seeing the twinkling of all the Christmas lights as he flew past the homes. He smiled as he imagined what the inside of their homes must look like. His ability to live in his imagination, create a world for himself that didn't exist, saved him. In his darkest hours he would escape there. This day, however, would be a good one for him.

There were bright lights set up around a corner of the fields. The warmth from that area felt unbelievably good to Arthur. He ran straight to it. A gentleman all dressed up approached him calling his name. This was quite unusual and scared Arthur. As he was getting to ready to flee, fearing he was in trouble for something, the rancher appeared. Arthur didn't know his name but liked him. This man was always kind, something he really appreciated.

He walked toward Arthur--broad smile, bright eyes and his hand outstretched. Arthur smiled tentatively and extended his hand, unsure why he was doing this. The rancher began shaking his hand vigorously and patting his shoulder at the same time. Arthur knew he must have done something right. He explained to Arthur that the local news stations had heard of this boy wonder--the young kid who was unstoppable and out working all the men. They were here to interview him and film him hard at work. The ranchers enthusiasm was contagious and Arthur was catching the bug. Though he would admit he did not quite understand what the fuss was about. This work was every day life for Arthur. He did it in his sleep.

Unbeknownst to Arthur, his story was aired and became the talk of the town. It gave hope to the hopeless and inspired many to give to those in need. Many parents gave an extra hug to their children that night as they tucked them into bed. The image of that young boy working so hard in the cold, all on his own - grieved many of their hearts. No one wanted to believe he was a lost cause.

A stranger approached the rancher and asked if they would sponsor a contest. The worker who picked the most tomatoes, quickest, would take home the jackpot. Nothing tugs at the heart strings more deeply than watching children suffer. This gentleman explained how concerned and touched many of them were after watching Arthur. He is so thin, young and dressed improperly for the bitter cold. They wanted to do something for him, if at all possible.

It was a normal morning, like any other, racing to work on the bike hungry and cold. Only this time Arthur felt the familiar butterflies fluttering in his tummy, except it had nothing to do with Juan. He begged any god that was listening to please keep Juan away today. He rarely showed up to work and this should not be the day to do so. He saw people lined up along the side of the fields. Some had signs and were waving and cheering. He waved back smiling, wondering what the signs said. The contest began...

Adrenaline peaking, Arthur moved at an unbelievable pace packing those tomatoes into one bag after another. He managed to do it ever so gently, not crushing any. He could vaguely hear the cheering and clapping going on because he was so focused. Whatever the jackpot was, he couldn't wait to surprise his grandma with it. He noticed she was moving slower and looking older. He really loved her and wanted to make her life somewhat peaceful. The thought of her not around suffocated him. It was hard to breathe, his pulse quickening. He knew she was the only one who was capable of caring for him. Wiping his eyes, he was grabbing another bag to feel up when a horn blared.

Arthur was amazed the day and contest were over. The rancher scurried up to him lifting Arthur's arm in the air and waving it around. It was done. He had won. A black bag was handed to him-filled with money from total strangers that he had won the hearts of...the smiles on all their faces looked genuine. They appeared so happy. He wondered why. All this for him? He was confused and overwhelmed. He didn't notice some of the moms and fathers wiping their eyes- he was busy now scanning the crowds for Juan. The number of people surrounding him surprised him and he was worried Juan might have heard about the contest. After all, nothing escaped his eyes. No one here would understand that being cold, alone or hungry were the least of Arthur's fears.

After many congratulations and hugs from total strangers, people started to disperse, including the camera crew and it grew quiet. Arthur was sitting on the ground, all alone, legs crossed one over the other. He wanted to revel in the moment, enjoy it all, even if he didn't grasp the enormity of it. He was clueless that he had touched so many hearts. As he started to get up, he could sense something. The heaviness set in and his legs became weak...he felt like an animal ready to be devoured by its' prey. Arthur turned around and Juan was standing feet from him. His body involuntarily flinched. Now when he needed all eyes on him no one was around. His mind was bursting with silent screams as he watched the rancher gesturing excitedly, describing how well he had done. The great pretender, Juan smiled, nodding toward Arthur as if he were also proud of him. As Juan walked toward him slowly Arthur put his head down, bracing his body for the blows he would inflict upon him. Instead he reached across and up, Arthur now taller than Juan, patted Arthur on the head and took the black bag out of his hands.

He didn't move for about 10 minutes, angry, sad and relieved. Shoulders slumped, the walk to his bike seemed like it took forever. The rancher yelled out, "good job," and went about his business. He rode through the neighborhoods with no emotions, shut down and empty. There were Christmas lights everywhere...Arthur promised himself he would not be so foolish again and allow himself to believe that good things happen. He would resign himself to live the life put before him without questioning it or hoping for more. Luckily for him, Arthur would find joy and hope in the smallest of things...

He had come upon several bunnies that were more than happy to make their new home in Arthur's wooden cage. He made sure to find scraps of food to keep in the cage. These animals meant everything to him. Arthur could love and provide for them, giving him a sense of belonging. Everyone needs to know they are valued somehow.

Chapter 19

A New Kind of Hurt

Arthur was having so much fun with all these little creatures making sure they were not cold or hungry. He even built a heating light for extra warmth. He did not notice how many bunnies had accumulated. It wouldn't have mattered. Arthur's instinct was to provide for anyone in need. It was all he knew. The sound of music caught his ear.

He put on an extra shirt along with the worn out but comfy, warm gloves the rancher had given him. The thought of that made him smile. For no reason at all, the rancher walked up and handed Arthur a pair of gloves one day after work. He is a nice man but Arthur couldn't help but wonder if he was the same guy behind closed doors. He walked out of the shed following the sound of music.

After walking about a block, he found them...there they stood--happy kids, colorful hats, glistening eyes, big smiles and shouting out music. Arthur loved the music. It was the nicest sound he had ever heard. Curiosity won him over. He walked up to the kids and asked them why they were singing. An older woman explained that they were Christmas caroling and invited him to join in. She handed him a small white styrofoam cup but Arthur was hesitant to take it at first. He couldn't resist it though. Warm, hot steam was wafting out of the cup and the aroma was enticing. He grabbed it gulping it down, looking every bit the deprived child that he was. Excitement caused him to shake. Maybe he would join the singing kids...the group moved on to the next house leaving Arthur standing alone with his now empty cup. A sadness slowly swallowed him up, deep from within, a yearning he didn't quite grasp.

His mind tells him to go home. He doesn't belong. Move. His feet numb, he stands still. The silent words sear. Arthur's world seems to be free falling and he feels so alone. Foolishness. He reprimands himself for allowing his thoughts to consider grasping onto a reality that would shatter if he mixed it with his world. Before he knows it, he is staring into the window of his own home. Juan is in the center of the big room. As if on cue, their eyes lock and Juan motions to him to come in. He has no choice and drags his feet slowly, one at a time, toward the one who controls the very air he breathes, or so it seems.

Drawing in his breath, the door creaks open, every eye on Arthur. He scanned the room trying to figure out why they were standing in a circle with Juan in the center of them. He sought out Grandma Concha looking for assurance, except she looked as confused as everyone else. His stomach turned over, fear gripping his insides. There was no avoiding it so Arthur turned to face Juan. He snickered and announced that he was ready to celebrate Christmas.

Arthur wasn't just shocked at his words, he also couldn't believe this was actually Christmas. They had never really celebrated this holiday before, or any for that matter. No one moved or reacted to Juan's words. But he definitely had their attention. As he started to move toward a black stuffed bag on the floor, Arthur stiffened, assuming Juan was going after him. Out of that bag came packages of different shapes, sizes and items.

Juan called each girl, one at a time, and handed them a gift. They timidly took it and got back into line, each one as unsure as the next what they were to do with the package. Lastly, Juan handed Grandma Concha and momma Mary small red boxes. Arthur stood there fidgeting, wondering if he should walk up to Juan. The young boy forgetting the about cruelties this man inflicted on him in his excitement. He looked around to see if there were anymore packages. Not able to contain himself any longer, he moved toward Juan and looked at him... a million questions in his eyes...but only one mattered and they both knew it.

With a sneering and smug expression plastered on Juan's face, he demanded everyone to open their gifts. Arthur knew, once again, that every eye was on him boring holes through him. It was silent except for the sound of Arthur swallowing hard. He felt it coming no matter how hard he tried to control it. His breathing became rapid, his nose started running and uninvited tears raced down his cheeks--exposing all he was trying to hide. From the corner of his eye he saw Grandma Concha moving toward him so Arthur bolted. He knew she would pay a price for trying to comfort him.

His face was hot from shame. Arthur couldn't stop the tears though. They came as fast as he was running. This hurt was different. He wasn't just angry or mad, he was crushed. It bothered Arthur that Juan could make him feel this way. All he wanted was to hate this man. Instead, it mattered more than the air he breathed to somehow gain or earn his father's love. Whatever was wrong, this young boy believed he was responsible for all the evil his father spewed out. It was debilitating to his soul. Exhausted emotionally, physically and mentally--Arthur sat.

The beautiful, clear lit up sky and festive homes clashed with how Arthur was feeling. The world felt dark, lonely and cruel. He wondered what each package held inside of it...Again, his tears flowed freely. Only this time there would be no shame attached to them. These tears cleansed his heart, mind and soul. Feeling the chill, Arthur rubbed his arms up and down quickly, looking for warmth. He spent the next few hours walking around enjoying each decorated house. It lifted his spirits. He started humming the music he had heard lately until he reached the garage. Wishing his bunnies Merry Christmas, Arthur curled up in the cot and closed his eyes, hoping for peace. Tears rolled down his cold, soft cheek as he drifted off to sleep.

Events in life have a tendency to propel one forward. We are shaped by these happenings, be it good or bad. Though time had passed and the chill in the air gave way to warmer days and nights, Arthur would not be able to forget that cruel Christmas night. He had lived with pain and hurt all his life but this was different. Something died within him and a bitterness had taken root. It threatened to destroy him. He would have to fight his own dark thoughts to keep from self-destructing.

Life was hard, yet it was monotonous. Nothing really changed much. Arthur worked seven days a week. He lived in constant fear of not meeting Juan's expectations. The nonstop burden of protecting and feeding his family wore on him. Arthur avoided home and Juan as much as possible. He didn't even care to see Grandma Concha, momma Mary or his sisters. He allowed himself to hate them sometimes. It felt better to live in anger. This helped dull the hurt. He could look at his family without so much emotional turmoil. Otherwise, he wept for his need of parents. Arthur was desperate for love and he cried for all he imagined he was missing...what he knew was that he was tired. Old, weathered and used up. It was as if he had already lived out a lifetime of angst, instead of just the 13 years that had clearly taken a toll on him.

Grandma Concha was quiet about most things but that didn't mean she wasn't aware of how Arthur was feeling. She knew he was avoiding them all and went out of her way to run into him. The walk home from work was quiet. He walked his bike so Grandma Concha could walk slower. He felt guilty as it was. After work she was standing there by his bike holding a paper bag. Excited, waving and smiling in her gentle way when he noticed her. Arthur's look said it all. No smile, no emotion, except possibly disdain. Her expression gave way to sadness, yet her eyes remained kind and soft. Without a word Arthur grabbed his bike and left. She followed behind. Why was he blaming her for Juan's atrocities? She was his everything. Even as they walked in silence, she allowed Arthur his own thoughts.

He didn't want to be mad or blame her anymore. His stubborn streak made it difficult to let things go, even when Arthur knew he was wrong. That stubborn streak also served him well throughout his life. It gave him the fight he would need to survive his life. He placed his right hand on her shoulder lightly, letting her know it was alright. She reached up with her left hand placing it over his. Arthur looked at her but Grandma Concha never glanced his way. She smiled and kept on walking. He wondered how she got to the fields. It didn't matter, their connection gave him a sliver of hope, allowing his mind to be still for a moment.

Arthur knew than that he would be different and not allow life to turn him into Juan. His thoughts had been so dark. A serious tug of war had been raging within him...fighting against Juan was wearing on Arthur. He understood by Juan's actions that he wanted Arthur to act like him. In his weaker moments Arthur had wanted to give in and join forces with Juan. He could share Juan's hate and anger for life, ending their private war. Arthur would be acceptable in his eyes...his soul cried out for something different though...

He slid her rough, weathered hand off his shoulder and held it tightly. Always a struggle for words when his emotions were bubbling over, he wiped his eyes and said sorry. As usual, Grandma Concha's warmth radiated from her covering him head to toe. Arthur started talking incessantly, tripping over his words. He was explaining how he was going to be strong. There would be no more stealing or anger taking over him. Arthur also promised that he would come around more often if he could, and take better care of her. It was as if he didn't say it quickly enough he would not be able to make it happen. She lifted his hand to her cheek, held it there shaking her head no. Grandma Concha caught the tears running down her face with their intertwined hands. She told him he did enough and to take care of himself. They continued in silence to their home. There were no words to make things right. Both of them felt a sense of relief for different reasons and a sense of doom but they smiled at one another as they went their separate ways...

Life with Juan was always evolving. His rules changed constantly, never quite sure what would set him off. His behavior became more erratic as he got older. Arthur watched him spend much of his time gambling, and he had more money than ever to gamble with. As the girls got older, Juan had his own personal working crew bringing in funds. Arthur knew they were making enough money that his family should never be hungry or cold but that was far from their reality.

Every day, as soon as Juan saw the girls and Arthur returning from the fields, he would yell at them to line up. Everyone stopped whatever they were doing and stood at attention. This man would intimidate Arthur, grabbing his very thin frame and shouting that there better be enough money for the family. Juan would than address his daughters, Mary and Connie(concha), screaming manically at them, that they better pay attention to how well he looked out for them...the little girls barely drew a breath, eyes wide open with a look of terror while watching their brother being tossed around. Arthur wanted to yell back, there is always enough but you take it all... Instead he took the abuse and always felt shame for letting this man destroy all of them.

When Juan believed he had their full attention, he would make each child turn in their money. Arthur was saved for last. Juan would hand him the cash and tell him to count it out loud. Never being educated he did his best. Of course it was always wrong. Juan would belittle him--calling him "stupido"(stupid fool) and kick him, literally, to the ground. Walking away with his head held high, laughing, Juan would grab his ever present beer and take a seat. Arthur didn't dare move until he sensed it wouldn't anger Juan. As he sat on the ground wiping his wet face with dirty hands, he was a sight to behold. He hated this man for never acknowledging anything he did. Arthur had made the very chair Juan was sitting in all by himself, after a horrible beating. In his mind he could picture that evening in detail...his thoughts took him to that night.

Juan had stumbled home drunk one evening and threw himself onto an old, wooden patio chair that was falling apart. Arthur always wondered where that chair came from... Juan came crashing to the ground with the splintered pieces of wood. Furious, he picked up a leg of the chair and dragged Arthur out of the garage where he slept. Bewildered and trying to figure out what happened, Arthur fought back while Juan swung that wooden leg hitting him anywhere he could. Arthur curled up trying to protect his face but couldn't stop the pain. He let out sharp piercing cries as Juan screamed unintelligible words at him. Grandma Concha came running out in a panic when she heard the primal screams and crying...she let out a gasp at the sight of Arthur. He was bloody--splinters all over his legs and his eye had a gash over it and was already swelling closed. It was one of the few times Arthur remembers his grandma ever begging Juan for anything.

Desperation reeked from her voice. He could see her though everything looked blurry. She was trembling, crying and pleading to go to Arthur and clean up his cuts. Juan murmured that she had a minute. Grandma Concha moved swiftly, kneeling down next to Arthur, pulling the over sized splinters out of his legs. She pulled his t-shirt over his head ever so gently and dipped it into the bucket of water that Arthur would wash up from. He closed his eyes hoping to banish the queasiness taking over his body. He could smell something medicinal and his body reacted to it, taking in deep breaths. Arthur uttered a loud piercing cry as she separated the torn flesh above his eye. Sniffling, her hands shaking, she cleansed it as gently as she could. Grandma Concha worried that his eye may have permanent damage. Juan pushed her away causing her to fall on her side. He told her time was up. She screamed at him that he was an animal...After grandma walked away, Juan calmly handed Arthur pieces of wood and told him to make him a new chair. Half naked, wet and cold, unable to stop shivering, Arthur spent the entire night building his father a chair out of wood pieces and metal. He ran back and forth until he found enough supplies to create something that would satisfy Juan. He never left Arthur's side, watching his every move and mumbling every time he approved...

Juan yelled for more beer bringing Arthur back to the present. He could see one of his younger sisters running over to grab the beer. This was the time to slip away unnoticed and Arthur did just that. Crawling away, he never looked back. There was a little window in the garage that he was able to jump through because he was so thin. Lying on the cot, scarcely breathing, Arthur could feel his heart racing. He placed both his hands over his heart to calm it down. It reminded Arthur of stories his sisters would tell him about how he always slept with his hands folded over his heart. It scared them because the girls always thought he might be dead...Terrified that Juan might walk in at any moment, Arthur didn't move from this position for hours.

The next time Arthur saw Juan, it was not what he expected. He was almost home from a long, hot day of work. Two of his younger sisters were running toward him. Suddenly he was no longer tired or hot, every nerve in his body alive and pushing him faster toward the girls. Palms sweaty, mouth dry, nervous stomach...fear...Arthur knew and understood fear better than anything else in life. He was dreading the answer they would give but he asked anyway, "what happened?" They simply told him that dad wanted him right away. It baffled Arthur that they could call him dad so nonchalantly. When Juan was around they had to call him by whatever name he demanded, but out of his presence--never. Arthur didn't think there was a word fitting for his father. Terms of endearment of any kind humanized Juan and Arthur knew better. He was certain there was not another human being as cruel or scary as this man.

Shoulders straight and emotions tucked away safely, Arthur approached Juan. Of course he did not speak but stood silently in front of Juan until his father allowed him to talk. Much to Arthur's surprise, Juan laughed and gave him a gentle smack on his shoulder. Unsure how to respond, he did not move. Arthur never took his eyes off of him because that always angered Juan, as did any signs of him looking weak or fearful, so it was difficult to stare into Juan's eyes. Arthur was terrified. There it was...that evil grin that started slowly at the corners of his mouth until it rested in his eyes. Juan handed Arthur a wad of money and told him to go visit the hooker that was waiting for him. Than he laughed again and left Arthur standing there. He exhaled, allowing all his fears to be released. Arthur finally moved and went to retrieve an extra shirt, a sheet from the cot and left. He knew better than to be found in the garage sleeping that night.

Many nights when it was more unsafe than usual for Arthur to be anywhere near Juan, he would leave and just keep going until he found open fields. There was plenty of farmland throughout Bakersfield. Arthur would set up camp there for the night. He would put on his extra t-shirt, spread out the sheet and lay down. Though he was alone, Arthur was not afraid out in the open. His fear was Juan. Loneliness, that was another issue altogether. He could not stop the tears...sobs that could be heard from afar if anyone had been near. At these moments, Arthur believed he could not take another day of this pain. He had never known any other life--

yet he craved love, kindness and acceptance. He shed tears for his grandma, his momma and his sisters. Crying is cleansing and exhausting allowing Arthur fell into a deep sleep.

Chapter 20

Just Another Day

Rest. Something Arthur noticed he was needing more and more of. He wasn't sure if he was sick or overworked. There was a gnawing pain in both of his legs. It didn't matter where he was, if he sat around to long, he would start to doze off. The work days were long but had never been an issue. Maybe it was the heat. Arthur believed the Bakersfield summer was the most intense, dry heat he could remember. Riding his bike home after a long day was very taxing on him. It surprised and worried him. Juan would not take kindly to that. Arthur decided to ask Grandma Concha for her opinion.

He jumped off his bike and walked to the shed first to check on his bunnies. The heat always worried him. Arthur had already previously lost 8 rabbits to heat exposure. It broke his heart. He gently lifted each one out of the cage and buried them. Life was cruel and most things did not make any sense to him. As he was shaking water all over the cage and bunnies, Grandma Concha walked in. Arthur jumped and dropped the bucket. He never had visitors in his sleeping quarters and it unnerved him.

As he slowly turned around, Arthur was greeted by a sweet smile.

The aroma was as nice a surprise as her presence. Grandma Concha was holding a cake. It resembled the ones he had seen in that ice cream/bakery shop. It was beautiful. He wondered why she had one... She held it up to him, her eyes brimming with tears, and quietly sang the sweetest song to him. Arthur averted his eyes to the cake and the flickering single candle in the middle of it. Grandma Concha was so emotional Arthur didn't know how to respond to that. She told him to make a wish and blow out the candle. He gave her a quizzical look and wanted to say no. But after realizing she was serious and excited, Arthur did as she asked.

Grandma sat on the cot and Arthur joined her. She explained, "this is your special day. It's your birthday--May 5th. On these days, people celebrate and eat their birthday cake." She handed him a fork and told him to eat. Arthur had to many questions...he blurted out his thoughts in his usual fashion, quickly and without waiting for an answer. "How do you know it's my birthday? How old am I? Where did you find this cake?" Grandma gently put her finger to his mouth and quieted him. She wanted to enjoy this moment with her grandson before it got interrupted by Juan. His curiosity was not easily quenched so she answered quickly. She told him in a broken voice, "I baked the cake and made the candle. I celebrate you every year and I think you are now 14 years old." Than the tears started and she couldn't continue. He had never celebrated a birthday before nor eaten cake like this. Even though there was sadness in the air, there was also a hope and joy surrounding them. Arthur couldn't resist and devoured a big portion of the dessert. It was all she hoped for and got up to leave.

Arthur knew she needed to go back before Juan noticed her absence so he mumbled with a mouth full of cake, "I am sick I think. I don't feel good lately." Grandma Concha sat back down and took his hands in hers, concern all over her face, and asked him what hurt. He explained about the pain in his legs and how he was always tired now.

Relief spread across her face. Grandma Concha stood up, holding Arthur by his shoulders, smiling and explained that he was growing. She made sure he understood all children experience growing pains. Arthur was in a talkative mood and nothing would have given her more pleasure than to sit and just listen. As she watched him, it hurt to know how alone he was. No one around to explain the simplest of things in life to her only grandson. The urgency to sneak back into the house gnawed at her. Without explanation Grandma Concha walked out. For that brief time Arthur felt loved and that he mattered somewhat.

He sat on the cot and finished the cake. Arthur was certain this the best meal he had ever eaten. Full and content, he laid back and thought about what she had told him. First, he wasn't sick, just growing. It made sense why Juan appeared to be shrinking and why his clothes had become uncomfortable. He couldn't wait until he wasn't so skinny. Arthur was embarrassed of his stick thin legs. He wondered if he should tell his grandma that he needed bigger clothes...she was already stressed, always struggling to keep up with all the growing girls. Secondly, Arthur couldn't believe he was 14 years old. He liked that thought. Maybe he was almost old enough to escape life with Juan.

It was a sobering thought as well. Arthur could not imagine life outside the constraints of his own existence. What would happen to his sisters...momma...grandma if he left? Would he see them again? He hardly ever saw Donna since she left. Arthur noticed that Ana was disappearing more and more often. He thought it odd that it was never mentioned though. Even Juan turned a blind eye, allowing her to get away with things no one else could have. Arthur rarely escorted Ana on any of her outings anymore. Why was Juan allowing that? Arthur figured something must be wrong with him as he thought back on the past week...

On his way home from work last week-Arthur took a detour and rode passed a school that he dreamed of attending. He had noticed lots of kids around his age always walking together in the afternoons. One day he followed the trail and discovered the school. On this day as he was walking around the building he saw Juan standing at the corner, holding a brown paper bag in one hand and watching him. Arthur was stunned to see him there and knew this was a mistake to be here. He waited. His feet felt like lead, dead weight and not moving. Juan never said a word or took a step toward Arthur. But he never took his eyes off of him. Juan lifted that brown paper bag and raised it to his mouth. As he took a drink, Arthur stared hard at Juan really taking in his appearance. He was so thin now and his stark white hair stood out against his olive brown skin. Something was changing about Juan. He walked away. Arthur could not pick up his bike quick enough. His hands were clumsy and he could not control his body from shaking. All that mattered was that he reach the house before Juan. Out of sight--out of mind.

As he lay there, his thoughts everywhere, he knew Juan's behavior was strange lately. It didn't make him any less terrifying but Arthur was relieved to see less of his father. Gaining some confidence as Juan appeared to be losing his, Arthur decided to ask Grandma Concha what she thought of him attending that school. It was a hope he couldn't let go of.

He knew dreams were not allowed to be a part of his life, yet his thoughts were consumed by them. Arthur was not alone in wishing, hoping and believing in more than he had--so did his sister Ana. She was friendlier, kinder and more thoughtful to anyone around her. The dark, ominous mood that she had sulked in for so long no longer controlled her. Arthur asked her why. Ana excitedly told him that she was getting married in a week. He was shocked that Juan was allowing another marriage. Than Ana told him they were going to tell Juan that very day. He admired her courage...it did not go well. Ana was not seen at home after that.

Juan went on a rampage. The whole week was chaos--fighting and screaming nonstop. Grandma Concha always went to battle for the kids. Arthur could hear her defending his sister. She tried explaining that there was no reason why Ana should not get married. The younger girls cried nonstop, frightened by the rage of their father. Arthur shivered knowing...waiting...contemplating running into Juan. He decided he would fight back this time.

Until it happened...Arthur had almost made it through the week. He was on his way to the shed to grab an extra shirt and hide out when Juan appeared. He had a board in his hand and was completely intoxicated. Slurring his words and stumbling around Arthur tried to dodge him. Juan swung the board at his son, catching the side of his head and face. Arthur fell to his knees--weak and dizzy. Juan found this funny and kept laughing, telling Arthur to get up and fight him like a man. He told him, "I want a man for a son, not a puto(faggot)." As he gained his balance and started to stand up Juan smacked him square in the face--breaking his nose. Juan hollered 'woohoo' clapping his hands together... Warm, thick fluid ran down from his chin to neck and spilled onto his shirt.

Arthur lifted his hand touching his shirt and looked at his hand...crimson red staining his fingers--sticky blood making him light headed. Arthur raised the other hand, pleading to Juan to be done. His head was throbbing and he needed to lie down. But Arthur needed his permission to do so. Out of character, Juan simply walked away. Arthur crawled over to his wash up bucket and immersed his face into it. He took off his shirt, soaked it in the water and placed it over his face. He laid back onto the dirt. Arthur gave into his grief wishing he could bury himself under the earth. He was tired of living.

The human spirit is strong. Arthur chose to put this incident behind him and move forward. The one thing he couldn't hide were the black eyes Juan left him with. He avoided his family as much as possible. Though people couldn't stop gawking at Arthur at work, or anywhere he went, not one person asked him if he was alright. He felt invisible and so alone. His sweet grandma waited by the shed on this particular day to let him know Ana would be getting married in two days.

Grandma Concha let out an audible gasp. Her arms wrapping around his skinny frame, she cried. Arthur hugged her tight, hoping to reassure her that he was fine. They sat on the cot as she examined his nose and cheek bones. Grandma walked out and returned immediately with some strong smelling green leaves. As she gently rubbed it all over his face, she told him about Ana's upcoming wedding.

Arthur asked where she had been hiding all week. Grandma Concha didn't know and didn't care. The important thing is that she was safe and soon to be out of Juan's reach.

Arthur looked at his grandma like she was crazy. He wanted to laugh out loud but would never disrespect her. He wondered if she just didn't realize that they would never be out of Juan's grasp. Disgusted, frustrated and instantly angry, he lay down on his cot and closed his eyes. Arthur wanted her to leave. Agitation was his friend and he welcomed it. He hated them all.

The roosters were crowing, the sun was rising and Arthur couldn't believe he slept through the night. He thought of his grandma hoping she knew he did love her. At certain times, he couldn't handle being near any of his family. Arthur wished he was totally alone and didn't know any of them. Until that thought really sunk in and panic would take over. Arthur would banish those wishes, afraid it would become a reality. He was so empty.

Two days came and went without incident. His face was healing slowly, he appeared to be on the mend. But his anger was mounting and he couldn't hide it. Surrounded by many sisters, two mommas and a crazy man--yet completely alone. His emotions and his thoughts were complex and so unpleasant. Arthur was angry...desperate to escape his own skin. That thought was daunting. Was it possible to ever live any other way? Arthur wondered if his two sisters were happy and if his mommas missed them.

As if on cue Momma Mary appeared. This was a rare occurrence. Apprehensive, uncomfortable and clearly sad, she was an open book. One always knew how Mary felt though she did her best to feel nothing. She looked around the shed examining Arthur's living quarters. He believed it was the first time his momma had ever been inside the shed since it became his home. She let Arthur know Ana was married but no one had been allowed to attend. He responded by nodding his head. Arthur was so bothered that his sister got married all alone, he couldn't stop his eyes from smarting. The silence was deafening.

Mary was quiet and withdrawn. Arthur looked at her for the first time in quite awhile. She was so thin and fragile looking. Her arms had bruises all over, as well as her bottom legs. His momma endured much and suffered silently. She was beautiful still, but there was not a smile left or any sparkle in her blue eyes. They were hollow, empty and lifeless. Juan had sucked the spirit out of his momma. Mary was an empty shell now. He knew she had quit believing in a life without fear. For better or worse, this was it.

Chapter 21

Hope Lingers

Somehow, someway, something always came through for Arthur at his most desperate moments. He will tell you that he believes angels had to be with him, or he would never have been able to survive his childhood. It still astounds him that he made it through that time in his life...anytime Arthur's thoughts focus on those painful years, he is immediately taken back to it and his emotions are raw. Luckily Arthur has mastered his thoughts as an adult, luckier yet, his 'angel' continued to appear in different forms throughout his young life. This helped him to push on and keep believing.

Grandma Concha(connie) would be his angel, his hope in Arthur's most dire moments. She was so upset after his last beating. Whether it was the broken nose, his double black eyes or the emotional exhaustion of it all, she let it be known by her actions just how angry she was. Though Connie only stood up to Juan a few times in her life, when she exercised that power, he listened.

Grandma Concha was determined to help Arthur experience some of his dreams. She had gone to the junior high school that he rode past everyday on his way to work. Arthur was signed up, enrolled and ready to join the eighth grade class. After she returned, Connie let Juan know what she had done. There was not even a thought regarding the consequences of Juan's wrath. Her anger was in control. The fury of a momma was not easily contained. So began another chapter in this young man's life.

Summer was coming to an end, though it was hard to judge by the weather. Bakersfield is known for its scorching, hot summer days long after the months of summer have ended. Arthur found ways to keep cool by wrapping wet rags around his head. But his mind was far away from work, the heat and the hardships of life. Dancing in his head was the vision of his first day of school. Arthur could hardly contain himself. He became that boy awaiting the excitement a new journey brought with it. Memories of first grade flooded his thoughts. He was certainly not afraid of the unknown. Expectations were high.

Arthur was not going to allow anything to ruin his school plans, not even Juan. As he got older, he became wiser. Arthur made sure to never show any display of excitement or affection toward things that mattered. It gave Juan such pleasure to take it away, knowing he was ripping Arthur's heart out. Never again. Arthur took extra precautions to avoid anything that might trigger Juan's cruel ways. His new thing was to destroy anything Arthur was involved with. One night while everyone slept, Juan took a bat and bashed his son's bike. Luckily it was still drivable. Another time, Juan went into the shed, opened up the animal's cages and left. Most of the bunnies were gone when Arthur returned from work, but a few remained. It made him smile, believing these few were loyal and loved him. He hid the these rabbits unsure when Juan would return and take them away.

He definitely knew something was not right with Juan's health. He looked sick, old and moved very slow, as if he was in pain. Every once in awhile, Arthur would find Juan's rags with dried blood on them. He mentioned this to Grandma Concha but she shook her head no emphatically, reminding him to mind his own business. Arthur was fine with that--just curious. He figured this must be why Juan was more apt to destroy his things instead of beating him. The anger he had learned to live with and hide so well was finding its way to the surface more and more frequently. Arthur was glad Juan was suffering and wanted to add to his pain. He had visions of beating Juan with the same rope, bat and board used on him without any remorse. Arthur also knew no amount of pain inflicted on Juan would ever erase the atrocities Juan put him through. So he let those thoughts fade away, forcing himself to think on better things.

Eighth grade. The thought of it no longer a dream but a reality. He was riding his bike to school after putting in three hours of work in the early morning. Arthur had no idea what he looked like, whether he was in style--an important matter at this age--or even if he was clean after working the fields. It didn't matter. The only thing he could focus on was his teacher. Arthur was excited at the idea of all the kids he would encounter but they were not his main concern either. Only the thought of his teacher loomed in his mind. She could ruin his school year. It was crucial that this teacher like Arthur. He jumped off his bike, pushed it up against the wall and followed the kids.

Arthur was nervous. Sweaty palms, a stomach ache and a parched mouth were in full gear. He swore he wouldn't forget but he did. Arthur couldn't remember the number of his classroom. Though Grandma Concha wrote it on a small piece of paper and stuffed it in his pockets, it didn't help. He couldn't read it. Arthur looked around at the scene surrounding him...friends hugging hello to one another, loud talking, and walking off together. Excitement in the air. Frustrated, Arthur looked to escape. To humiliated to ask anyone to read what the paper said he walked out to the fields. This was his comfort zone--green, beautiful, peaceful and alone. He remembered this field packed with students kicking around a ball or running laps in the past. Today, thankfully it was empty.

A loud, shrilling bell goes off, jarring Arthur from his thoughts. Watching all the commotion, students scurrying off in different directions, he didn't notice a man approach him. Arthur jumped to his feet, explaining as quickly as he could that he was lost. This rather large man standing before him unnerved Arthur. He trusts no male figure. This gentleman sets Arthur at ease when he kindly asks him which classroom he is looking for. Arthur hands him the crumpled white paper and they are off. He tells Arthur that his name is Felix, bringing a smile to his frightened face and that he is the yard duty. Felix explains that he keeps an eye out for everyone's safety and to come to him with any problems. Arthur thanked him and walked into his new classroom.

This new school year would be a coming of age for Arthur in many ways. He would see the horrors of his life in a different light. Arthur was becoming a young man and escaping to his make believe world was not so easy to come by anymore. He fully understood the tragedy his life was and sorrow filled his soul. Yet, there would be glimpses of hope that somehow there was a better life awaiting him. His deepest need to love and be loved drove him-- stopping him from giving up. Only Arthur could decide which path he would choose...

Things at home were the same but somehow eerily different. Juan was in control of all things still, yet there was no disguising the changing of the tides. Juan was losing his stronghold on the family slowly but surely, or he no longer cared as much. Arthur couldn't figure out whether it was voluntarily or if life was paying Juan back for all he had done. The older girls could come and go more often on their own, as long as they worked the fields first and turned in their money. Juan would still berate them, bellowing out words like "whore" and "tramp" anytime they walked out the front door but he didn't get up to chase anyone. As a matter of fact, he rarely left that patio chair anymore, sleeping there often. Arthur would watch Grandma Concha or momma Mary help him up and walk Juan to the house. Sometimes he wondered why they did not just leave him there, but he knew why. It wouldn't be worth the price they would pay for neglecting this vile man.

Every morning as Arthur jumped on his bike, eager to get to work so he could race to school afterward, he would hold his breath. Quietly he would ride past the porch praying that Juan wouldn't be sitting in that chair. Looking into his eyes, with that wicked grin always caused Arthur to tremble. He believed Juan had no heart and being forced to face him was like looking into the face of evil. The older Arthur got, the more he realized how vulnerable he was around Juan. Arthur went to great lengths to avoid him at all times.

School was exciting and much more fun than he imagined it would be. Arthur liked his teacher, Ms. Harris. She was kind, patient and laughed often. Her sweet smile captivated him. He always wondered what great things went on in her life that made her so happy. Arthur wished he had a momma like her. Something about her let Arthur know she understood how frail his heart was...and that he was worn out before his day began. If he could have hung out with her all day, while Ms. Harris attempted teaching him eight years of missed schooling, Arthur would have found school to be the ideal setting. Of course that was only another dream not to be.

Meeting all the new kids was a challenge for Arthur. There were always so many questions he couldn't answer. Such as, "which school did you come from?" "Where do you live?" "Can you hang out after school?"... Than there was the problem of clothing. For the first time, Arthur realized how important it was to dress nicely and be in style. Grandma Concha did her best to make Arthur's clothes stylish from any material she could find and he wondered where she found his ugly shoes. He hated them but was grateful to have any shoes and without holes. Arthur was uncomfortable and felt like an oddity. He looked nothing like the other kids. Some laughed behind his back at his appearance, but there were those who would tell him he looked like a hobo. He wasn't sure what that word meant, though he was certain it wasn't good. Those who weren't as vocal would stare at Arthur with pity in their eyes. Arthur knew and understood that look. He'd rather be made fun of...so he decided to hang in the classroom more often foregoing the social part of school. He was comfortable as the loner. This was a normal way of life for this young boy becoming a young man. There was one thing however that Arthur couldn't resist--music. He was always fascinated by it and music would draw him out of the classroom. His teacher took note of that.

Ms. Harris introduced Arthur to the band teacher, Mr. Jordan. Though Arthur's life was tumultuous at best, and full of despair, this became a magical time. Music filled his soul and gave him a purpose. Mr. Jordan gave him the opportunity to join the band. He was pleased how musically inclined Arthur was. Unlike schoolwork, music came naturally. Arthur could not believe Mr. Jordan handed him a trumpet to take home and practice on. He didn't have the courage to tell him that it wouldn't be possible to take it home. Arthur knew Juan would destroy it simply because it was his, so he hid it in his desk when class would end. When it became apparent to Mr. Jordan that there was a problem, he offered a different position to Arthur. He was now a proud member of the baton team leading the marching band. Arthur could not wait to share this with his grandma. It was something Juan would never know.

Arthur raced home as quickly as he could, while balancing his baton and new uniform. His excitement to share this news with his grandma was uncontrollable. He was giddy and clumsy, dropping things as ran. His treasures tucked away safely in the shed Arthur quietly snuck into the house through the back window hoping to find Grandma Concha. There she was on her knees, scrubbing away any dirty spots on the floors that all the kids left behind. A serious offense to Juan which would lead to a serious beating if he found any... Seeing Arthur's lit up face, she stood up, ready to share in his joy. He dragged her to the shed. By the time she got there his enthusiasm was so contagious she was laughing. She needed this, not able to remember the last time she laughed. Grandma hardly heard a word he said, enthralled with his smile and wild gestures. Words were spilling out of his mouth so quickly he had to keep repeating himself. Not wanting to cast a cloud over his joy, she simply hugged him, her tears wetting his cheek. She warned him of the importance of being careless around Juan and not to be fooled by his indifference now. It frightened Grandma Concha imagining what would become of her little boy. She begged him to hide the uniform and baton with care and not allow Juan to catch a glimpse of either. Arthur knew better. The baton would become his beating stick. Never.

School events came and went. Arthur was not allowed to join them. Work interfered in most cases, but more importantly, Arthur was terrified of Juan finding out about anything he was doing. It was risky enough every time the band performed and Arthur showed up for that. He marched proudly though. Arthur says there are no words to convey how special he felt. It did not matter to him that no one could be there to watch him. Belonging to something such as this group was an emotional and surreal experience for him. This opportunity would have a huge impact on his life giving him the emotional and mental strength to fight for his survival.

Chapter 22

Survivor

Running late for a performance because of work, Arthur got careless and forgot to check for Juan. Rolled up and stuffed into a little bag on his back were his baton and uniform. He didn't race past Juan's spot quietly or quickly as usual. Preoccupied with thoughts of leading his marching band Arthur never saw Juan standing off to the side. With one swift movement Juan yanked him off of his bike. Everything scattered. His uniform and baton sprawled across the gravel. Juan gave Arthur one hard kick near his rib cage area. Than he walked over to the uniform, put his foot on it and rubbed it into the dirt. The look on Juan's face was one of disdain, contempt and hatred. He held up the baton looking at his son and laughed, calling him "puto" "cavron" and "stupido." He tried snapping the baton in half but could not... Juan threw it at him and started walking way. Arthur was a walking time bomb emotionally, mentally and physically, he snapped. He jumped up screaming and charged at Juan. It stopped Juan in his tracks, taken aback, he moved out of Arthur's way. He continued screaming, "no, no, no," loudly and violently, picking up anything he could find and throwing it. Than he stopped. Arthur looked Juan right in the eyes while picking up his uniform and baton. The coldness, hatred and contempt seeping out of Arthur's heart, along with his tears, could not be hidden...it took over his fears. He quietly told him, "don't ever touch me again Juan or I will kill you."

Arthur jumped on his bike and took off never looking back. As he pulled up to the school he saw the band in full swing, performing without him...he vowed to never allow Juan to interfere in his life again without a fight. He knew this was a turning point for him. It scared him a little. No longer able to silence the screaming inside his mind, something had to change. This sadistic man had finally pushed Arthur beyond his limits and it was showing. Grandma Concha had noticed the change in Arthur's demeanor. His edge and tension reminded her of Juan sometimes. This broke her heart. She warned him as often as she could that he prolong his suffering by hardening his heart.

Arthur continued to enjoy school. He found marble tournaments and joined them. He knew he was outstanding at this game. Arthur won all 30 games throughout the course of the school year. Kids who once made fun of him or avoided him, now sought Arthur out. They wanted him to teach them his skills. He enjoyed showing off and being accepted, but at the end of the day, Arthur was alone, empty and seeking love. He was conflicted, bitter and angry at himself for still wanting his father's love and approval. Arthur tried to sleep, sobs overtaking his body. He didn't want to sleep in this ugly, cold, dirty shed anymore. Every once in awhile the loneliness was overwhelming. Why did Juan hate him so? An unanswered question that would haunt Arthur all his life...

The more quiet and withdrawn Juan became, the more Grandma Concha and momma Mary catered to him. Even some of Arthur's sisters were going out of their way to make sure Juan was alright. It sickened Arthur. Why couldn't they see he was manipulating them all? Even in their kindness toward Juan, he berated them. He would always control them making Arthur wonder why he wanted Juan's approval.

The school year was coming to an end. Arthur had not learned to read or write, though he gave it a valiant effort. More importantly, he had met teachers who believed in him. Arthur knew somehow these teachers figured out his situation was not good. It was never discussed but every so often one of the teachers would show up with clothes, baked goods or shoes. This should have made Arthur happy, excited or thankful--instead he would feel defeated and hopeless. He knew he would never have someone who cared like his teachers and this would end along with school. At this age, Arthur had realized he could never continue on to high school. He could not do what it required--read or write.

Arthur's band teacher, Mr. Jordan, wanted to honor Arthur for his effort and hard work throughout the year. He understood how difficult this young man's life was. Mr. Jordan had enjoyed and appreciated Arthur's eagerness to learn. He was shocked to discover a few months into school that Arthur was illiterate. This kind teacher made sure the other students never found out. Arthur hid it well. Graduation day was upon them. It was a sad day for Arthur.

He watched and listened. All the kids were running around excited...talking about their summer plans. Everyone was also signing yearbooks and talking about the high school they would attend. Arthur avoided this scene and waited in the gym where the ceremony would take place. Students and parents finally started filing in. Lost in thought, Arthur was confused and surprised to hear Mr. Jordan call his name. Embarrassed, he walked up to the stage trying to straighten his wrinkled clothes and comb his hair. He has a very stubborn cowlick in the front of his hair by his forehead and he knew it was out of control. He was stunned when his band teacher handed him this shiny, gold award. Speechless, Arthur reached his hand out toward Mr. Jordan's extended hand. Instead this man pulled Arthur in and gave him a big hug. Unable to contain his emotions Arthur wept. He exited the stage quickly, eyes focused on the floor.

Try as he might, Arthur could not control his shaking. Adrenaline was coursing through body and he couldn't shake it. He sat on the ground next to his bike and stared at the trophy awarded him. Arthur tried to remember every kind word Mr. Jordan said about him but all he could focus on was this big, burly man hugging him. It was the first time Arthur could remember a man ever hugging him. He felt safe and unafraid, wondering if that's how it could have been with his father. The thought of the award meant nothing. It could not love him or keep him safe. Anger surged within him. Arthur gave into the anger, sadness and hollow feelings enveloping him and by the time he arrived at his house, he was all cried out.

Grandma Concha was waiting in the shed. Always faithful to show him he was loved and not totally alone. She jumped up and clapped as he walked in, smiling and congratulating him for graduating. She was painfully aware of how out of touch she really was regarding Arthur's life. There just were not enough hours in the day to give him time, nor was it worth the beatings they would face for spending time together. There was a red balloon floating in the corner and another beautiful cake. In spite of how Arthur felt this made him smile. He used to dream of owning a balloon once upon a time. Life had caused his dreams to diminish slowly, one at a time, until they were almost completely forgotten. She sang happy birthday to her grandson and cut the cake. Handing him the balloon she hugged him and said she was so proud of him. They sat quietly, sharing a sweet but sad moment in time together. Grandma didn't even try to stop her tears... The thought of him alone at graduation hurt to much. He consoled her the best he could and than asked how old he was. Grandma Concha smiled through her sadness touching his face, as she loved to do, and said, "you, my son, are 15 years old--a young man now."

As he watched his grandma walk out he noticed her limping a lot. Arthur wanted to ask her if she was feeling alright but words wouldn't come...his thoughts, feelings and words did not seem to come together as easily anymore. Nothing made much sense nowadays. Even the neurotic, crazy life Arthur was used to had changed. There was no longer a rhythm of any kind to his days. Arthur was really surprised to hear his age. His thoughts were all over the place. How did he get to be that old? Was this it for him? He took off walking and didn't return for the night.

Arthur found a deserted spot near the fields, laid down and stared up into the peaceful sky. This felt good, familiar, and right. His anxiety subsided allowing Arthur to fall asleep. He returned here for the next few weeks each night for comfort. With his world changing, Juan sick and both his momma's slipping away, Arthur was seeking familiarity. He was hoping to feel grounded somewhere.

He could feel the intensity of his glare. Arthur wondered if Juan was hiding somewhere nearby and why? He did not show up at the fields anymore but Arthur knew he was out there somewhere. As he wiped the sweat dripping from his forehead into his eyes, he looked around nonchalantly. It was already heating up, the good ole Bakersfield summer. He knew he could count on that. Arthur could not shake the uneasy feelings that had settled on him. He was anxious to go home and check on his grandma and momma as soon as possible.

It had been a few weeks since Arthur had seen his family. Of course he saw some of his sisters at work but curiously missing were some of the younger ones who had started working along with momma Mary. As he stared at the surroundings of his home he felt apprehensive. Arthur hated it. Everything about this house made him feel unloved, unwanted, and worthless. He wanted to quickly check on everyone, leave his hard earned money in Juan's jar and take off. But as soon as he saw Grandma Concha his heart softened. Though he did not want to be responsible emotionally or physically for any of them anymore and he dreamed of creating a new life for himself, Arthur couldn't abandon them.

She smiled, so happy to see her boy. It pained her that Arthur had chosen to disappear from her life but she understood. Grandma Concha did not know how to help or comfort him. As she hugged her grandson, she told him that he had grown again. Arthur towered over his sweet grandma. He was surprised at her appearance as well. Her hair was all white and it appeared that she had shrunk. Grandma Concha did not look strong or brave enough to contend with Juan anymore. In truth, their appearances were not that different from a couple of months ago, but the time apart caused them to really take notice of one another. Their connection was strong and they missed each other much more than they dared to admit. Giving into their emotions was lethal, Arthur avoided that at all costs.

Arthur did go into the house to check everyone out. Some of his younger sisters were excited to see him but his concern was his momma. Than he saw her. Momma Mary was putting a white cloth, dripping with water, around Juan's neck. She turned sensing someone's presence. Mary knew better than to draw any attention to her son so she turned back to

Juan. Arthur watched her for a bit longer. His momma still looked young but tired and lifeless. He had seen enough, things were very much the same.

He told his sisters bye and went looking for his grandma. She knew Arthur was taking off again and wanted to stop him. Grandma Concha told him, "we need you to be around, please sleep in the shed." Arthur was angry, hurt and surprised that she would ask that of him. Without a word he walked off to the dark pit they called his home. She tried grabbing his arm to explain her reasons but Arthur pushed her hand off of his, uninterested and bewildered by their gentle treatment toward Juan. As days passed, it did not take long to realize something serious was wrong with Juan. Grandma Concha nor his momma said a word but they were nervous and spent all their time around him. Arthur had every intention of asking what was going on. After a couple of weeks of waiting, before he had the opportunity to ask, Juan approached him. He was standing in the shed waiting for Arthur. Upon seeing him standing there, Arthur became that frightened little boy...sweaty palms, stomach turning, and parched mouth. Juan's affect on him angered Arthur.

This was it. Arthur decided to take a stand. He clenched his fists, walked right up to him--as close as he dared--and told him, "I'm not afraid of you anymore, so get out." Gaining confidence with his adrenaline rush Arthur got louder and louder until he was screaming, "get out" over and over again. Arthur never noticed Juan move to the side and grab a board. Weak and sickly now, he was barely able to swing the board and catch Arthur's lower leg causing no pain. But it still angered Arthur and he lost control, throwing everything in his way and yelling loudly, "leave us alone."

Connie and Mary came running with all the commotion. Trailing behind them were all the girls. No one moved when they realized it was Arthur out of control instead of Juan. It was quite a sight to behold. He looked like a wild animal devouring its' prey--eyes filled with rage, his hair going every direction and surrounded by all the stuff he was tossing. Shock registered on every face. Arthur sunk to his knees filled with shame as he saw the look of terror on their faces, knowing he was the cause of it this time. Moments passed before he looked up, everyone was gone.

The next morning momma Mary was waiting. Arthur was happy to see her until she unleashed on him. This mild, timid woman was angry at her son. Mary grabbed his ear, explaining that he would never behave like that again toward anyone. She left him standing there with his mouth open. Yes, his ear hurt, but his confusion was her anger. She never showed him any emotion and this would be the time she would choose to do so...protecting Juan? The betrayal welled up within him and he couldn't stop the flood of emotions. He packed the few things he owned and knew he would never return to this place again.

Arthur avoided his sisters at work staying on the other side of the fields. There was plenty of workable farmland making it easy to stay hidden. After a couple of weeks passed, Arthur wanted to go home, feeling so alone. It bothered him that no one, not even Grandma Concha, looked for him. He wondered how long it would take for them to notice he was gone.

Chapter 22

The Door Closes

He didn't have to wonder for to long. Two of his sisters came running toward him the next morning, upset and crying. They told Arthur to be quick that grandma and momma needed him immediately. He dumped his bike and took off on foot. Arthur had outgrown the bike long ago. His legs hit the handle bars, making it impossible to move quickly. He was in full panic mode by the time he arrived at the house. It was empty. There was blood on the living room floor. Arthur ran through the house, the yard and the shed calling out names. He almost knocked his sister down in his haste. Alicia told him to follow her to the hospital. He did not need to wait, he had ridden passed it often. He could not imagine what had happened. In all their years of strife, they had never gone to the hospital. He tried catching his breath as he stared at this building housing the sick. Arthur dreaded walking in the doors.
Arthur knew exactly which direction to go, he followed his sisters wails. His feet could not move

fast enough. One of the girls was hysterical, begging someone not to go away. Than he heard her say, "we won't know what to do without you dad." His footsteps slowed down as he started to realize they were here for Juan, not for his grandma or momma. He leaned against the wall, sliding down to have a seat outside Juan's room. There were tears and Juan mumbling to the girls. A kind nurse pulled Arthur up smiling and gently nudged him into the room. She told him it was important that he go in and say his good byes. His other two sisters arrived just than. Juan smiled at everyone and told them to sit. It was very crowded--two momma's, 12 girls and 1 boy all gathered together in this spot.

He was furthest away from Juan, sitting on the floor watching the scene unfolding before him. Arthur felt numb and nauseous. The younger girls were hanging onto Grandma Concha in one corner, the older girls standing around Juan's bed and momma sitting next to Juan holding his hand. She looked straight ahead, no emotion registering on her face. They stayed like this for hours. Finally Juan spoke. One by one he called each daughter to come to him.

He took their hand in his, telling each one to take care of their momma and each other. Juan went on to apologize for everything. Most of them wept. One of his sisters became hysterical, hugging his neck, begging him not to leave. Juan tried to comfort her and gave her his scarf. There were not much words he said to Connie, nor did she hold his hand. At last,

Juan called Arthur to his side. Not a kind word, not an apology, no chance for closure...instead, he told Arthur to work hard and that his life was to be lived for the girls and his momma. Before he would leave Arthur asked Juan, "did I ever do anything right? Why do you hate me? What did I do?" His only response would be, "get out cavron- out of my sight." Those words hurt in a way he never imagined. There would be no acknowledging Arthur as a worthy human being, even on Juan's deathbed. He walked stiffly out of the room and sat by the door. Arthur wanted to scream, cry, anything...but he was numb.

For the next hour or so Juan pleaded with Mary to forgive his sins. She refused, telling Juan to ask God for forgiveness not her. Juan's breathing was labored but he was relentless, begging her. On his deathbed, as in life, Juan got his way. Mary conceded, forgiving Juan for all his evil ways. Within minutes, Juan closed his eyes and ceased to exist. They all wept, each for their own reasons. Arthur could not figure out why any of them would be sad. He believed they were crying tears of relief. He knew his tears were a mixture of that, along with the unanswered questions that burdened him. Arthur knew he'd never have answers now. He must bury those thoughts along with Juan. No one moved or spoke for a long time, Arthur finally went home alone to the shed and cried himself to sleep.

Juan was buried without a ceremony. Arthur wondered if it was his momma or grandma that handled it. Grandma Concha made everyone wear black every single day after his death. She explained that it showed honor and respect for the dead. Grandma also made Arthur move into the house. He was not happy about that. He felt like a stranger milling about. Though Juan was gone, his presence was felt everywhere. Arthur would sneak out at night, often, to sleep in the open under the stars.

There were no happy kids running around or joyful noises. So much damage had been done, it was like walking into a war zone after the battle was over. This Rodriguez family did not know how to carry on. They were walking corpses. Arthur did notice his momma give more of an effort to interact with his sisters. Mary even became somewhat affectionate, but only with the girls. Arthur's presence made her retreat back into her shell. It broke his heart to realize she had no idea how to live around him. The awkwardness was staggering. Grandma Concha also noticed. She went out of her way to show Arthur love. Connie(concha) understood how devastated he was by Juan's last words to him. Her grandson appeared more lost now than when Juan was living. At least there had been an order and purpose in their bleak existence.

Life was exactly the same several months later, as if Juan were controlling them from the grave. Nothing changed. They each went to work, came home, put their money in the jar, ate dinner and went to bed. There was an ominous dark cloud over them and no one seemed able to walk through it to get the other side. Arthur was scared, afraid to let go and enjoy anything. Time did not seem to be his friend, healing was not coming easy, if at all. His only joy was his grandma.

He made a point of spending time with her every day. Some days it was just their presence spent together that made life bearable. Arthur's respect and love grew for his grandma. She cried often, seemingly unable to control it. Her emotions had taken on a life of their own. Grandma Concha was always apologizing for the destruction of all of their lives. She worried him and he wanted to give her hope. Arthur tried to find ways to make her understand they knew she had no control over it. But the breakdown between mother and daughter, Connie and Mary, did not help the matter. It ached to the core of her soul. Her grieving heart had not escaped Arthur's eyes. His momma was rude and cold to Grandma Concha. Mary avoided being around her. Arthur was very protective of his grandma and he wanted to say something to her but he could never hurt his momma, ever. She had suffered enough. Instead, he made it his mission to put a smile back on his grandma's face, focusing on that for the next few several months.

Winter was upon them and it cold. Arthur raced from the fields to a farmer that was giving away wood. The rancher watched him load up his arms with all he could carry. This man offered to help Arthur knowing he was on foot. But he declined his help because no one was allowed at the their house. So the rancher told him to come back later for more. Arthur thanked him and took off. He was so excited to surprise his grandma. The house needed warming and he knew it. All the girls complained about it. Arthur was tall and very thin but strong from a lifetime of field work. Yet the wood was heavy and getting the best of him. Arthur arrived at the shed and was arranging the wood when he heard loud sobs. Throwing the wood down, he went running, crashing through the front door. All eyes turned to Arthur but it was his momma who eventually went up to him and just stood there. He almost yelled out 'what' in her face but he refrained.

Her cheeks were stained with dried tears and puffy, red eyes causing her to look 10 years older. Voice trembling, hand shaking as she put it on Arthur's shoulder whispering, "momma is gone. She left us this morning." Fresh tears running down her face, she walked away unable to comfort her son.

Arthur could not breathe. Confusion and chaos, he did not understand. He wanted to ask what happened to her but words wouldn't come.

Somehow he ended up in his old room—the shed. He curled up on the cot and went to sleep. Days went by, Arthur drifted in and out never leaving the shed. Until the ceremony for his precious grandma. He went through the motions but vaguely remembers the service. Arthur spent the couple of weeks in the shed shutting everyone out. He wouldn't allow anyone in. The minister stopped by to talk with Arthur but he was not receptive. He did let Arthur know that his grandma died peacefully—her heart just stopped. He laughed at the idea of her death being peaceful…he knew she never had a peaceful day.

Of course it made sense to Arthur that her heart would just stop. Juan had almost killed his grandma emotionally, mentally, physically and his momma finished her off. It was all to much to bare. Arthur wanted to see and hug her one more time. Some of his sisters checked up on him and tried encouraging him to go back to work.

Anger. This was Arthur's only friend. Raw, strong and consuming. His rage pushed him out of the shed and back into the world but not to work. Arthur did not care anymore, about anything. In those few weeks he let his plants die, released all his animals and did not check on the girls or his momma. He didn't even know what or if his family was eating. There was nothing left to give. Contempt, irate, furious. indignant--these words described the only emotions left in this young man. He had an aggressive anger ready to explode.

On this particular day, Arthur set off aimlessly, nowhere to go and with no purpose. He looked how he felt--angry, dirty clothes and uncombed hair. It didn't take long and it certainly didn't take much for Arthur's wrath to surface. In truth, he was looking for trouble. It came in the form of a young girl and guy arguing. This was none of his business but it did not matter. He walked up to this young couple in the middle of a lover's quarrel. He pushed his way between the two and told the guy to leave her alone. This dark haired beauty panicked, jumping to her feet quickly, trying to explain that she was fine. If fell on deaf ears. Within seconds, Arthur and this nameless guy were throwing punches. This stranger had no idea what he had gotten himself into. Arthur jumped on this opportunity to release his rage. He could not see through his tears but he kicked and punched wildly. Arthur didn't hear the screaming of the girlfriend or notice the crowd gathering until the sound of a loud whistle.

Throbbing hands, bloody knuckles, ripped shirts and a bloody guy on the dirt not moving--all the makings of a violent fight. Arthur stared at this scene and was appalled that he caused it. The policeman told the crowd to disperse. Another man was helping carry the wounded young man to the grass. Arthur could hear that pretty girl crying as he was being handcuffed.

He couldn't control his own crying. The officer gently put Arthur into the police car. The drive was silent. When they arrived at the station, he told Arthur that life would be difficult if this was the path he was going to choose. Arthur agreed. He asked Arthur for a number to call his parents. He described where he lived as he was put into a cell and they removed the cuffs. He was that frightened young boy again-- alone and upset with himself. How could he have done this? Arthur grabbed the small blanket off the metal bench covering his head and didn't move for hours.

Stiff, cold and sore Arthur stood up to stretch. It was very quiet. There was not a person in sight. He wondered how long he would sit in this cell. It was sticky and warm in here and he was filthy. Dirt dried on blood dried on dirt--a mess. An officer walked in and asked how he was. Arthur had no answer, he didn't know how he was. The guard left a tray of food on the shelf, leaving Arthur alone with his thoughts. Normally ravenous with an unending appetite, he couldn't master the energy to eat. Arthur couldn't even gather his thoughts. He wanted to be unafraid, be able to dream and have a hope that wasn't always torn apart. Arthur closed his eyes, leaned his head back and tried to think of happy moments with his grandma. He wondered if Christmas had come and gone since her passing. He knew cold weather meant Christmas time. Different memories played over and over in his mind of their time spent together. The slamming of a door brought Arthur to his feet.

His eyes opened wide in shock, not at just the fact that she was standing there, but more at the look on her face. Momma Mary looked fierce. Arms folded across her chest, Mary told him, "get out of there."

The officer unlocked the cell and moved out of the way. Arthur didn't get the chance to step out of the block--his momma was on him in a heartbeat. She slapped him twice hard, once on each cheek. Arthur's face stung but not as much as his shame. Mary set him straight telling Arthur, "this is the only time you will ever be in here. Nothing will bring her back. What would she think of you beating someone? Go home, go to work and be proud of how live your life each day." The officer bid them a good day. Arthur followed his momma out of the station--head down and silent.

The situation was never really addressed again. Arthur wondered if his momma ever told his sisters that he not only beat someone up but also ended up in jail. The thought of it all caused him deep humiliation. Arthur knew he would never go back to jail again. He attempted to apologize once for his behavior but Mary would not allow it. She went on to explain to him that it was done. The past is the past. If he intends to survive in this world, he needs to look forward. His momma told him, "regret only leads to bitterness." Mary walked away. It was the most conversation those two had engaged in that he could remember. Arthur was very surprised by her sternness and how quickly she took over as the leader of the household. One thing he was certain of--his meek, mild, timid momma was a thing of the past.

Bewildered, Arthur had no idea how to move forward. He couldn't accept that Juan left without apologizing or letting him know that he cared at all. It pained him. Than unexpectedly Grandma Concha is gone...to much to bare. He seemed to only identify with rage, anger and violence that threatened to take on a life of its' own. He needed air. Arthur walked for a long time. He came upon a beautiful field of endless green grass. Just looking at it helped him to relax. He searched for the right spot where he would spend the evening.

Stretched out, breathing deeply and staring up at the sky--Arthur told his grandma how much he missed her. He could hear nature talking...he had forgotten how beautiful it sounded. Arthur was vulnerable, emotionally fragile and tired--so very tired of being angry, hurt, and alone. His chest felt so constricted from holding it all in. So he stopped trying to run from his pain. Every emotion he buried came pouring out like a rushing river and it was cleansing. He talked and cried without taking a breath for hours--letting his grandma know everything he felt. All talked out, Arthur listened to the silence. He sat up and asked Grandma Concha, "please help me." His hope was tied to her. No one had taught Arthur about how to live a better life so he was scared. He wasn't even sure there was a person living now that was able to care about him.

Arthur got on his knees the way he remembered his grandma used to do in her most frightened times, folded his hands and bowed his head. Lost, he wasn't sure where to begin. So he quit thinking about it and faced his fears. Arthur said, "I'm going to trust you like she did please don't leave me alone." After what felt like an eternity, he opened his eyes and waited. He sat back unsure what to expect or what to do now.

As the evening grew still, Arthur lay back into the welcoming arms of the earth. In his weakness, he was drawing strength. A deep euphoria swept over him. Relaxed, content and hopeful--he smiled. Mystified by his desire to survive, Arthur inhaled the beauty around him and looked forward to a new day.

Life has a way of intertwining one's soul forever to its' past. Arthur--a young man on the brink to adulthood--determined, hopeful and soft hearted would give his all to break free. Fighting hard to leave behind that world of pain, fear and shattered dreams--the battle began. His soul had been crushed from the weight of it. A cleansing was needed from the inside out. Arthur was going to triumph over everything, every disillusionment, every disgust in life.

It did not escape him that he was physically free from bondage. Uncertain how to free his thoughts and begin his new life, Arthur decided to put an actual plan together. He needed order and structure to his day in order to function. Tired, worn and frightened from the strength it takes to breathe, but sure of himself, he started by announcing his plans to his momma and sisters.

Arthur told them, "I'm no longer wearing black to honor Juan and you shouldn't either. He is controlling us even though he's dead." His momma's demeanor changed. Her body language showed that she did not like him telling her anything. Mary's presence had a way of breaking Arthur down, causing him to retreat to that young lost boy. Though he became emotional and his voice trembled, he knew it was now or never. Arthur stood up straight, drawing courage from the hope dwelling within and spoke with certainty.

"I don't have the answers I'm looking for...I will never know why Juan hated me so much...I don't know why you are uncomfortable around me...I'm not even sure what love is supposed to be. But I'm going to find out. I've carried that burden all my life. I'm going to see the world through new eyes. I want that joy I see in other people." The more Arthur talked, the more he believed what he said. "I will not be numb anymore. I won't allow anyone to stop me. I will take care of you momma but I'm going to live. So whether or not you agree with me, or think I'm not taking care of my responsibility, I will do what I need to do to change my life."

Chapter 23

At Last

Arthur didn't look back. He seized every opportunity to absorb life. This change started at the place Arthur had grown to despise. He looked around and decided his family would live in a place that he was proud of. Arthur bartered work in exchange for painting material, wood and plants. He spent every free moment, including weekends, repairing and restoring the place he would finally call home. This took months to complete. The restoration not only took place with the house but within Arthur as well. He was happy with what he accomplished, especially the yard and garden. No longer afraid or hiding anything from Juan, his garden flourished. The girls and his momma liked what they saw. His journey had just begun. It would be an emotional and mental battle that Arthur faced head on. Where he was once blind, now he could see.

There was kindness in the world if you were open to it. Though the relationship between this loveless family softened as time went on, the barriers that divided them had taken root on solid ground. Each would try to mask the damage they carried but it was a burden they would shoulder alone. Arthur and his momma could not break down the wall that time had built between them. He watched with envy and longing as she interacted with the girls, ever so gentle, and what appeared to be carefree. He wanted to know what she was really thinking. Arthur knew his momma was adept at masking her feelings, much like him.

As time went on, he chose to remember the few good moments of his childhood, if only a few. In an instant, Arthur learned how powerful his thoughts could be--destructive or calming. He had the ability to choose. The things his mind couldn't accept, Arthur put to rest. Even Arthur's outer appearance took on a softer, more gentle look as his love for life grew. The scared, angry young boy was becoming a fine young man. His greatest desire was to share the love growing within him.

Each day as he set off to work Arthur had a purpose. He looked for the woman who would be his family. Someone he could love and who might love him back. It was a thought that consumed him. He was ready and capable to start life on his own. He continued the field work but also picked up odd jobs earning extra money. Arthur put some of it away for himself and used the rest to change his family's life. Arthur wanted to restore some of what they had all lost. He took each sister at different times and bought them proper attire. There was always plenty of food in the house now too. This young man felt more than just the responsibility of material things, he wanted to give them hope. The older girls continued working, some in the fields and some in other areas. Arthur was very happy that his younger sisters were going to school. It was surreal. For the most part, Arthur was pleased and believed the best was to come.

There were days, out of nowhere and for no apparent reason, Arthur would succumb to fear. His mind would go back to the time Juan ruled them and panic would take over. He would hear over and over 'stupido... you aren't loved...you're useless...worthless'. Arthur would have to work very hard to calm his thoughts and climb out of that pit. Thoughts of Grandma Concha would relax him. He would choose to believe that she loved him. She thought he was worth something. At those moments Arthur desperately wanted to be loved...

The lonelier Arthur felt, the more he worked. He held several jobs at once and stayed busy. Arthur was outgoing and quite talkative making friends easily. His past was not discussed with the new circle of friends but most people had heard of it. Strangers would never know the path he had walked--Arthur was full of charisma and life--covering the emptiness he felt. He shared that only with the stars at night when he was unable to sleep. Though he was a young man now, tall and handsome, many nights Arthur would take a blanket and fall asleep outside where he was most comfortable. He would remind himself that what is past is gone and to keep moving forward.

Life was simple. Time moved quickly, months turning into years. Arthur couldn't remember how long his grandma had been gone. He thought of her often. Arthur did not spend much time at home. In spite of all the changes, being there made him feel very alone. If he wasn't at work, he was out. Arthur immersed himself in the night life. He would attend the town dances and hang out at the drive-in with the guys. It was the perfect opportunity to whittle away the hours and meet new people.

As outgoing as Arthur was, he was shy with the girls. He had many girlfriends that he'd spend time with. But Arthur never opened up to any of them. He certainly never took any of the girls home to meet his family. When Arthur would go home and pay attention to each sister, he was surprised how quickly they were growing up. Each one doing their own thing, just like him, searching to somehow fill that gaping hole in his soul...This family, splintered and irreparable, yet peacefully existing with one another. The facade continued--filling up his free time with meaningless relationships. It was important to not have idle time. He wondered if loneliness would plague him his entire life.

Than one day everything changed. In an alleyway, of all places, Arthur saw her. A quick glimpse of this petite, fair skinned, dark haired beauty. He was on his way home from the fields and quite dirty. She was laughing and talking with another girl in front of a liquor store. Arthur caught her attention by staring and it startled her. She took off quickly without a backward glance. Though it was unclear- something had begun...he was mesmerized by her presence. He felt the same stirrings as when he had held each new baby sister- the hope of life...

Arthur was determined, not easily swayed. He knew there was something different about her. Arthur says she had a look and move about her that he couldn't get out of his mind. She had such a grace about her. This young woman had no way of knowing just how relentless he could be. He showed up in the same spot until he saw her again. Arthur tried talking with her, asking her name over and over. She ignored him until she couldn't. Laughing at his insistent behavior, she responded by telling him her name--Gloria. He liked it and was grateful her name was different than his 12 sisters. She went on to explain, "my father doesn't allow me to date or have guys over, so please leave me alone." With that said, she walked away. It only fueled Arthur's desire to know her. He couldn't wait to run into her again.

As chance would have it, that happened soon after their last encounter. Arthur was dressed and ready, waiting for his friends to show up and leave for the dance. He took one last look in the mirror making sure his outfit was in order. Arthur was meticulous with his clothes. After growing up in rags, it was more than important to him. Hearing the horn blare, Arthur took off shutting the door quietly behind him. He knew his mom did not approve of him going out every night by the look she would give him. But Arthur refused to sit still and let that house become a life size coffin. Walking out, he took a deep breath of the fresh air, looking forward to the night.

The dance was in full swing as the boys approached the hall. Arthur remembered a time not so long ago when he sat outside these dances waiting for his older sisters. He was glad those days were gone. Arthur leaned against the wall content to people watch. She went flying past him, laughing with girlfriends. Arthur couldn't believe Gloria was here. He went up to her without a word and whisked her off to the dance floor. She tried resisting him with every reason she could think of. Gloria told him she needed to stay with her sister and girlfriends. She also explained how much trouble she would get into if her father knew. But Arthur had an answer for every excuse. Finally, Gloria relented and spent the evening talking and dancing with Arthur. They danced beautifully together. He impressed her.

As the evening came to an end, Arthur knew what he wanted. This spirited, happy, beautiful young woman was going to be his wife. She had no idea these thoughts were swarming in his mind. He wanted to walk her home so he could spend more time getting to know her. Gloria told him absolutely not with such force, Arthur agreed. She was so relieved that she scribbled her phone number on the piece of paper he handed her. Arthur watched her get into a car full of people and couldn't wait to call her.

Getting to know her better was going to be much more difficult than he expected. Arthur had to go find pay phones to call her and when he did, Gloria was rarely home. He daydreamed about her during his working hours and went out at night hoping to see her. They did run in the same circles loosely. They were able to spend unplanned evenings together hanging out at the drive-in, as well as a few more dances. After weeks of talking off and on, Arthur told her he wanted to take her on a date.

Gloria was nervous and told him her father didn't allow her to date guys he didn't know. That's all it took. Arthur asked around until he found out where Gloria lived. She had no idea the turn her life was about to take.

Arthur showed up at Gloria's house, anxious to meet her parents. He would do whatever it took to win them over. The time he had spent with Gloria gave him so much hope. He wasn't going to let his fear of men scare him away. He knocked on that front door, introduced himself and declared his intentions. Arthur told Gloria's father, Moses, that he was in love with his daughter and wanted his permission to date her. Impressing this man, Moses welcomed Arthur into their lives and spent the next few hours talking.

Gloria was surprised at Arthur's audacity but even more shocked at her father's response. She was quietly elated. Gloria had fallen as quickly for Arthur as he had for her. She loved his need to be loved. As their relationship blossomed, his love and respect grew for her. She was full of grace and cherished him in the most gentle way. Arthur had never felt complete or loved like this. She trusted him completely and that thought was daunting. So many memories he had never shared with her, it terrified him that he might let her down. He knew he would never be alone again though. Gloria had given him the gift of love that he had been denied all his life.

The love and warmth he yearned for would finally be his. Arthur proposed to the woman that completed him. They had met, dated and were married within nine months. Though he would battle mental and emotional demons throughout his life, Arthur would live to realize all his dreams. His life would find him surrounded by the woman he pursued. The love of his life, Gloria, would give him five children that adored him. The unconditional love he would shower on his children was admired not only by them but by anyone who knew this family. Arthur couldn't believe this woman and children were his. It was salve to his wounds. Love was the hope that fueled his dreams.

Arthur would inspire strangers and friends by his drive and love for life and his family. He would be a trailblazer and an inspiration to family, friends and strangers alike. He never had the opportunity to attend school again but Arthur started his own very successful contracting business with his wife by his side. This allowed him to help out all his sisters and momma at different times in their lives. But his focus in life would remain his own family. Arthur took nothing and no one for granted. He appreciated life.

It is life changing to watch someone triumph over ones adversities, simply because the power of the human spirit is resilient. The heart is the seat of all emotions. Arthur did not want to live with the ghosts from his past and all his failures. He chose to believe in himself when no one else did. That simple yet difficult decision gave him the faith he needed. Instead of allowing the tragedies of his life to bury him, he broke free, refusing to give in to it. This little boy lost dared to live life and he was set free.

The Rodriguez Family- waiting for the last baby-Sam

Made in the USA
San Bernardino, CA
28 March 2013